Dear Reader,

Welcome! Would you like to raise a child who's mad about books? Then this is the guide for you.

At Dubray Books, we believe that reading is one of life's great pleasures. We also believe that books can enhance and even transform a child's life.

I've never forgotten the books my parents and grandparents shared with me when I was a child, the books I read by myself, and the teenage novels that have never left me. From Richard Scarry's BUSY, BUSY WORLD, to the subversive wit of Roald Dahl, to the longings of Judy Blume's Margaret in ARE YOU THERE, GOD? IT'S ME, MARGARET. Not to mention the raw teenager voice of Holden Caulfield in THE CATCHER IN THE RYE which stopped me in my teenage tracks and made me a passionate reader all over again.

I've been involved in children's books all my working life and there's no better job in the world. Along the way, I've discovered hundreds of amazingly talented illustrators and authors, both Irish and international, and now I would like to share this knowledge with you.

I was a very poor reader in school; I only learned to read fluently at nine. If it wasn't for my parents' persistence, reading to me every single day and sharing the joy and excitement of really good books with me, I would not be where I am today.

So share your own enthusiasm for books and reading with your child. Sing nursery rhymes and lullabies to your baby, share picture books with your toddler, read aloud until you're practically asleep in the bed beside your six-year-old. I firmly believe the right book, in the right child's hand, at the right time, can change their life.

Are you ready to discover new friends and revisit some old ones?

Let us begin...

Sarah Webb
Children's Book Consultant

P.S. Our must-have books are marked with a star. ★

Howard

Illustration reproduced by permission of Walker Books
© Niamh Sharkey from *I'm a Happy Hugglewug*

BOOKS FOR BABIES AND TODDLERS: AGE 0 TO 18 MONTHS

As Dorothy Butler, a wise and experienced New Zealand children's bookseller, once said 'Babies are never too little to look.' You can share books with even the youngest children and there are lots of wonderful board books designed with small, tearing hands in mind. Above all, keep their first book experiences fun.

Invest in a good nursery rhyme collection and sing and read to your tiny one. Nursery rhymes are part of their literary heritage and don't forget to include all your own childhood favourites. Look at the end of this section for some nursery rhyme book ideas.

Leave their books within easy reach. A book box on the floor or low level bookshelves is ideal.

So here's what to look out for in a book for a baby or young toddler:

- Small, baby-sized books that little hands can deal with – even quite young babies can learn to turn pages.

- Strong, well designed books that can withstand a beating or a biting, or in the case of plastic books, even a bubble bath.

- Clear, uncluttered pages with bright, attractive colours, or striking black and white. Avoid fussy books with too much action on the page.

- Illustrations and images that a baby will recognise from everyday life – pets, people, cars and trains.

Hug Board Book
by Jez Alborough
Walker Books €7.70

This was one of my daughter's very favourite books when she was small. It's a sweet, simple story about a little baby chimp who has lost his mum. All the other animals in the jungle have someone to hug but where's *his* hug? The text is made up of three words – 'hug', 'Mummy', and 'Bobo', and it's the perfect book to share with a baby.
Also by this author: *Duck in the Truck*

The Very Hungry Caterpillar Board Book ★
by Eric Carle
Puffin €9.25

This classic picture book is a must for any baby's book box. The story of a hungry caterpillar that eats his way through all kinds of delicious food, leaving a small hole behind in the pages to be explored by tiny fingers. The simple, well written text and gloriously colourful illustrations combine to make an unforgettable first book.
Also by this author: *My Very First Book of Colours*

Dear Zoo Board Book
by Rod Campbell
Campbell Books €7.70

A delightfully simple lift-the-flap board book with rounded edges. This classic book has been a favourite with children for over twenty-one years, and rightly so. It's a charming story about a child who writes to a zoo, asking for the perfect pet.
Also by this author: *Oh Dear!*

Opposites: Charlie and Lola
by Lauren Child
Orchard €7.70

Lauren Child has won many awards for her collage picture books for older children. This board book is perfect for babies and toddlers. It features her original, quirky artwork and is a treat for the eyes, a stylish book that will be enjoyed by children and parents alike.
Also by this author: *Numbers; Things*

Click, Clack, 123
by Doreen Cronin
illustrated by Betsy Lewin
Simon and Schuster €9.25

'1 farmer sleeping, 2 feet creaking, 3 buckets piled high, 4 chickens standing by.'

The simple text in this board book gently rhymes and there is a strong narrative which builds as the animals gather in larger and larger numbers. The surprise at the end will charm and delight.
Also by this author: *Click, Clack ABC*

Van Gogh's World of Colour
by Baby Einstein
Scholastic €7.70

Each page of this board book reproduces a different Van Gogh painting and features a different colour. It's a clever idea, a book that keeps both baby and parent interested and a good way of introducing art to young eyes. The Baby Einstein books are educational but, more importantly, fun – look out for other great titles in this range.

Also by this author: *Mirror Me!*

Where's Spot? ★
by Eric Hill
Puffin €7.70

I've never met a child who doesn't love Spot, the mischievous puppy. This is the perfect first book. With a very simple hide and seek story, flaps to lift and clear, bright pictures, this title makes story time fun, again, and again, and again! Start reading it when they are small and they'll still enjoy it at age three. A real winner.

Clap Hands
by Helen Oxenbury
Walker Books €6.15

Helen Oxenbury's classic board books contain babies that are bald, smiling, clapping and playing. They are irresitible for other babies and toddlers and feature a wide range of different coloured babies doing just the kinds of things that babies love doing. The illustrations are simple, bright and just right for tiny eyes.

Also by this author: *Say Goodnight; All Fall Down*

The Rainbow Fish Bath Book
by Marcus Pfister
North South Books €7.70

Books can also be enjoyed in the bath. This charming story about sharing is set underwater, very apt for its padded plastic bath book format. The Rainbow Fish has sparkly holographic scales on his body and the illustrations are colourful and friendly.

Ouch! I Need a Plaster
by Nick Sharratt
Scholastic €6.15

Young children are fascinated by plasters. This fun board book is clever and subtle. The young reader can count out the plasters using Sharratt's strong, colourful illustrations. The text is written in clever rhyming verse, just right for reading out loud. A charming counting book for any tree climbers or budding doctors!

Also by this author: *Ketchup on Your Cornflakes*

Fuzzy Yellow Ducklings
by Matthew VanFleet
Ragged Bears €15.40

All my children have grown up with this wonderful touchy-feely book. Each page brings a new surprise under its larger than average flap. From koalas to iguanas, the animal illustrations are unusual and striking and the book also introduces the concept of shapes in a fun way. A real winner and a great gift for a new baby.

That's Not My... Board Book Range from Usborne
by Fiona Watt
Usborne €9.25

This Usborne touchy-feely range is great for tiny exploring fingers. With bright, child friendly pictures, solid thick board pages and simple text, these charming books make reading fun. There are over eighteen in the range, featuring cars, dinosaurs, princesses and many other topics. Pick to suit your child.

Owl Babies Board Book ⋆
by Martin Waddell
illustrated by Patrick Benson
Walker Books €7.70

Martin Waddell is the master of the well crafted picture book and this strikingly illustrated book works well in the smaller board book format. The story of three baby owls who are waiting for their mother to come home with food, it's a reassuring tale and with its lush, dark illustrations, a real visual treat.

THE LADYBIRD BABY AND TODDLER COLLECTION

Ladybird board and cloth books are highly recommended for their quality and value. Every baby should own at least one. They also publish useful nursery rhyme collections.

Baby Touch Picture Book
Ladybird €10.75

A large-format board book with the extra interest of split pages. Each page is filled with touchy-feely and shiny panels to keep young babies and toddlers amused. A good book which makes early reading fun.

First Cot Book
Ladybird €7.70

An ideal very first book that can be used from birth. A concertina-style cloth book with strong, bold black and white images and a mirror for baby to look in. Pop it in your baby's cot or pram.

Photographs © Walker Books

All About Leslie Patricelli

Leslie lives in Seattle, Washington, with her husband, Jason, her three children, Beck, Tia and Tatum, not forgetting the cats, Sassy and Elvin. She says her favourite food is spaghetti and she likes to wear jeans most of the time. As well as writing and illustrating her great 'baby' board books, she has designed and animated for Microsoft and is currently working on some animated shorts for Playhouse Disney. She says second to playing with her kids, writing and illustrating books is her favourite thing to do. Luckily for us.

All About Niamh Sharkey

Niamh Sharkey graduated with first class honours from the College of Marketing and Design in Dublin. In 1999, she won the prestigious Mother Goose Award for best new illustrator and she has gone on to win many subsequent awards for her distinctive work.

Niamh lives in Skerries, North County Dublin, with her husband, Owen, and three young children, Megan, Oscar and Aoibhe, and Rosie the cat. She loves dancing, walking by the sea, playing with the kids, and playing jazz piano (very badly she says!). She also adores feta cheese and olives. Her favourite picture book at the moment is *Don't Let the Pigeon Drive the Bus!* by Mo Williams.

If she wasn't an illustrator, she'd like to be an Underwater Scuba Diver Photographer.

Yummy Yucky Board Book ★
by *Leslie Patricelli* Walker Books €7.70

Although this is a fairly new book (2004), it's one of my all time favourite board books. Each page is carefully designed with witty pictures and bright, eye catching colours. The text is very simple – 'Spaghetti is yummy, Worms are yucky' – but it never fails to make me and the kids smile. And isn't that what good books are all about?
Also by this author: *Quiet Loud; Blankie; Dummy; Big Little; Binky; The Birthday Box*

The Ravenous Beast Board Book
by *Niamh Sharkey* Walker Books €7.70

A stylishly illustrated book for toddlers and younger children. The ravenous beast is hungry; he's hungry, hungry, hungry. But is he the hungriest animal of all? 'Nonsense smonsense,' scoff the other animals, and 'Hokum Pokum!' They claim to be even hungrier. Great fun to read aloud, Sharkey's quirky, brightly coloured illustrations set it apart from a lot of other board books. Fun for adults and children alike.

Also available in a book and DVD edition which is highly recommended.

NURSERY RHYME COLLECTIONS

Every baby should own at least one nursery rhyme collection. Nursery rhymes are part of a baby's literary heritage and should be passed down from generation to generation. It always makes me sad when children say they've never heard of Humpty Dumpty or Incy Wincy Spider. So enjoy singing and sharing them with your baby and toddler!

Michael Foreman's Nursery Rhymes
Walker Books €20.00

A delightful collection of all the old favourites and some less well known rhymes too. The watercolour illustrations by award-winning artist, Michael Foreman, are a joy to look at and to share with a young child. Available in hardback and paperback.

The Orchard Book of Nursery Rhymes
illustrated by Faith Jacques
Orchard €20.00

A charming, traditional hardback book of nursery rhymes with detailed illustrations which will interest an older child too. Jacques researched her costumes using illustrations from the late 18th century, giving her work a very authentic feel and making it enjoyable for parents who are interested in history. This book makes a lovely birth or christening gift.

Round and Round the Garden
by Sarah Williams
illustrated by Ian Beck
Oxford University Press €12.30

A charming book and CD set featuring lots of favourite nursery rhymes and action songs, from Incy Wincy Spider to Row, Row, Row Your Boat. Gentle, colourful, child friendly illustrations by Ian Beck make this a good book to share with young children and toddlers alike. Includes useful step-by-step illustrations to the hand and body actions for parents and minders.

If you can't remember all the tunes to nursery rhymes, why not invest in a nursery rhyme tape or CD for the house or car? The BBC produce a good range of nursery rhyme tapes and CDs including:

50 Favourite Nursery Rhymes
BBC/Cover to Cover € 7.70

TODDLERS AND YOUNG CHILDREN: AGE 18 MONTHS TO 3+

Introduction

It's important that you as parents, grandparents, godparents, aunts and uncles enjoy your reading experience as much as your child, so we have chosen books we know you'll love too. After all, you may end up reading the books dozens if not hundreds of times if they become much loved favourites, as we hope they do.

Toddlers adore picture books. At Dubray Books we love our picture books. While other bookshops are cutting down on their ranges, we are building ours up. There are some wonderful new authors and illustrators out there such as Oliver Jeffers and Emily Gravett, and the old favourites such as Shirley Hughes' delightful Alfie books are still going strong.

Here's what to look out for in a book for a toddler or young child:

- Picture books with excellent, strong and clear illustrations – vary the different kinds of art work you share with them – from Lauren Child's strong colours and collage, to Oliver Jeffer's carefully designed watercolours, and the more gentle paintings of Helen Oxenbury

- Funny stories – young children love a good belly laugh and it's good for adults too.

- Books with lots of jaunty rhyme and repetition – great fun to read, great fun to listen to.

- Books that make reading fun – pop-ups, lift-the-flap books, touchy-feely books, and yes, even noisy books.

Each Peach Pear Plum
by Janet and Allan Ahlberg
Puffin €7.70

This clever rhyming picture book has delighted children for over twenty-five years. Children will have great fun finding the fairy tale characters hidden in the pictures and adults will enjoy reading the well-written and jaunty text aloud.
A great book to share with older toddlers.
Also by this author/illustrator team: *The Baby's Catalogue; Peepo*

Goodnight Moon (Board Book)
by Margaret Wise Brown
Campbell Books €7.70

A young rabbit prepares for bedtime, saying goodnight to everything. The illustrations are very strong, with blocks of arresting, lurid orange and green alternating with monochrome pages; the text is strangely lyrical and soothing. I'm not sure why this book works but it does. Share it with your own little bunny and see.

The Baby Who Wouldn't Go To Bed
by Helen Cooper Corgi €7.70

A picture book charting every parent's dilemma, the restless baby. The baby drives his little red car through an amazing fantasy world of huge toys until he finally starts to get sleepy. A gentle story with vibrant illustrations, just right for bedtime.
Also by this author: *Pumpkin Soup*

Hairy Maclary from Donaldson's Dairy
by Lynley Dodd Puffin €7.70

Hairy Maclary is a scruffy little dog who gets into all kinds of trouble. The bright, humorous illustrations are just right for younger children and look out for my favourite character, the little dachshund, Schnitzel von Krumm 'with his very low tum'. Wonderful stuff, with lively rhyming text for reading aloud.
Also by this author: *Slinky Malinki; The Other Ark*

Silly Mummy, Silly Daddy
by Marie Louise Fitzpatrick Frances Lincoln €9.25

Beth is in a bad mood and her whole family try to snap her out of it by entertaining her with sock puppets and rather dubious works of 'art'. The text is simple and quick to read, good for tired parents at bedtime. A highly successful book for moody toddlers, with eye-catching illustrations.
Also by this author: *Silly School*

Alfie's Feet ★
by Shirley Hughes
Red Fox €7.70

Shirley Hughes has produced some brilliant picture books in her day, but this one is my favourite. It's the story of Alfie, an enchanting but normal four-year-old, and his new wellies. A sweet, rather old fashioned story that is a joy to read aloud, perfect for any child who loves puddles and splashing about.
Also by this author: *Alfie Gets in First*

Guess How Much I Love You ★
by Sam McBratney
illustrated by Anita Jeram
Walker Books €9.25

A delightful picture book about a big and a little nut brown hare who try to measure their love for each other. The gentle illustrations by Anita Jeram in muted shades of pink, brown and green are wonderful. A lovely quiet book to share at bedtime.

Brown Bear, Brown Bear, What Do You See?
by Bill Martin
illustrated by Eric Carle
Puffin €9.25

This bright and breezy picture book will capture the imagination of any toddler. The rhythmic text is fun to read aloud but it's the larger than life collage illustrations by Eric Carle (of *The Very Hungry Caterpillar* fame) that really bring this book alive.

Little Owl and the Star
by Mary Murphy
Walker Books €7.70

This is one of my favourite Nativity books. It features a young owl who is sitting in a tree with a 'waiting feeling' until a star leads him to a very special stable. The illustrations by Irish author/illustrator Mary Murphy are stunning. A treat for all the family, especially at Christmas.
Also by this author: *I Like It When*

Meg and Mog
by Helen Nicoll
illustrated by Jan Pienkowski
Puffin €7.70

This classic picture book has been entertaining children for over thirty years. Children love witches and Meg and her cat, Mog, are brought to life by Jan Pienkowski's bold illustrations with their strong colours and clever use of black outlines. A feast for young eyes.
Also by this author: *Meg's Eggs*

We're Going on a Bear Hunt ★
by Michael Rosen
illustrated by Helen Oxenbury
Walker Books €9.25

A charming picture book which combines action packed illustrations with simple, repetitive (but never boring) text. A dad and his four young children stomp, squash and splash through fields of grass, rivers and muddy lanes on a 'bear hunt' and then get chased home by a real bear. Another excellent book for reading aloud.

I'm a Happy Hugglewug
by Niamh Sharkey
Walker Books €9.25

This book, by award-winning Irish author/illustrator Niamh Sharkey, features the Hugglewug family of colourful monsters. The artwork glows, and Sharkey cleverly introduces some useful concepts like numbers and colours in an unobtrusive way. A fun book to share with any child of two plus. **Also by this illustrator:** *The Gigantic Turnip* (written by Tolstoy)

Dinosaur Roar
by Henrietta and Paul Strickland
Ragged Bears €7.70

A fantastic book of dinosaur opposites with zany, larger than life illustrations in bright primary colours. 'Dinosaur sweet, Dinosaur grumpy; Dinosaur spiky, Dinosaur lumpy'. An excellent book for sharing, especially with lively boys.

The Elephant and the Bad Baby
by Elfrida Vipont
illustrated by Raymond Briggs
Puffin €9.25

This wonderful picture book isn't all that well known but it's one of my favourites. The Bad Baby meets a kindly elephant who lifts him onto his back and takes him 'rumpeta, rumpeta, rumpeta all down the road'. The unusual illustrations are by Raymond Briggs of *The Snowman* fame. A hidden gem.

Farmer Duck ★
by Martin Waddell
illustrated by Helen Oxenbury
Walker Books €9.25

'There was once a duck who had the bad luck to live with a lazy farmer.' This is a brilliant picture book, full of jaunty repetition and great fun to read aloud, especially if your farmyard animal noises are up to scratch. Fabulous illustrations by the always wonderful Helen Oxenbury. 'Animal Farm' for toddlers! **Also by this author:** *Pig in the Pond; Snow Bears*

Photograph © Random House

All About Shirley Hughes

If Lauren Child is the picture book Princess, then Shirley Hughes is the Queen. With over fifty books under her belt and an OBE for services to children's literature, she is one of the best loved author/illustrators ever. Born in 1927 in West Kirby, her first book was *Lucy and Tom's Day* in 1960. Since then she has gone on to win all the major awards going and has created some of the most enduring characters in picture book history, Alfie, and Lucy and Tom.

She based her characters on first hand experience gained as she raised her own young family. As she explains "at that time... there weren't many books for young children about real life – what it feels like getting up in the morning, going to the shops, having lunch and so on." In 1977, Shirley won the Kate Greenaway medal for *Dogger*, another tale of an ordinary and yet monumental family incident – the loss of a much-loved toy.

"My books have grown out of real situations with which very small children can identify," she says, "perhaps even at an age before they can fully appreciate fairy tales. They are mostly set in a city background – my own part of London to be exact. The domestic details are very local and English, but I hope the themes are fairly universal. I would like to think I draw with sentiment but never with sentimentality. Family life is a high drama, not a sweet idyll." And so say all of us.

A Note on Character Books

Toddlers and children of all ages love characters, from Dora the Explorer to Thomas the Tank Engine. They find character books familiar, friendly and reassuring. There is a wide range of character books available in all our shops. Character books keep children interested in books, but are not always all that well written. Remember to vary their reading and to introduce lots of different books, not just character books.

The Mr Men and Little Miss books are popular with children of two upwards. There is a book to suit every child, from Mr Tickle to Little Miss Sunshine.

Angelina Ballerina is one of our favourite characters. The Angelina Ballerina books are ideal for any little girls who love to dance and are well written and charmingly illustrated.

Angelina Ballerina
by Katharine Holabird
illustrated by Helen Craig
Puffin €9.25

Angelina is a feisty young mouse who loves to dance. Set in Mouseland, this book combines witty text with magical, very girly illustrations. Ideal for budding ballerinas.

Introduction

This is a glorious time for young readers and their parents. Most children are starting to decode words and print, in books and on road signs, cereal boxes and anything they can get their hands on. They will have story time in playschool and school (if they don't, then ask why not?) and will be interested in all kinds of different books.

It's a magical time for reading aloud too. Find books that both you and your child will enjoy. And remember, you can share books with them that they wouldn't be able to tackle on their own – like the shorter Roald Dahl titles – so check out the books marked 'Read Aloud' in the Age 5 to 9 Years section on pages 31–49.

And remember to include some of their old favourites in your reading – they may still like Spot and please don't tell them they're too 'old' for Spot and need 'big boy/girl books'. They may find their old books comforting.

It's a great age to introduce fairy tales, and there are some great collections reviewed after the picture books (Fairy Tale Collections). No child should grow up without meeting Rapunzel, Hansel and Gretel, Goldilocks and all the magical fairy tale characters. You'd be amazed at how many children are only familiar with the Disney characters like Cinderella and Sleeping Beauty.

Try to set some time aside every day to read to your child – even 5 minutes at bedtime makes all the difference. And always give the message that books are fun. Don't force books on them if they are not in the humour. They will find their own way on the reading journey.

So here's what to look out for in a book for a 3 to 5-year-old:

- Funny books – children of this age love humour. The Lauren Child picture books are entertaining for both children and parents alike.

- Books on tape or CD are wonderful for the car. Or put them on in your child's bedroom while they are playing. Again, they can listen to books they wouldn't be able to read for themselves – my four-year-old has been a Dahl audio book fan for over a year now and also enjoys listening to THE WORST WITCH by Jill Murphy.

- Pop-up and novelty books are another great way to make reading fun – there are some wonderful pop-ups reviewed after the picture books (Novelty and Pop-Ups), like Sabuda's stunning version of the WIZARD OF OZ.

- It's a good idea to run your finger under the text on the page as you read to your child – this way they will start to associate the squiggles on the page (the letters) with the meaning in the story. A gentle way to introduce the mechanics of reading to young children.

Where's My Teddy?
by Jez Alborough
Walker Books €9.25

Eddy goes into the wood to find his teddy and suddenly comes across a huge teddy. Along comes a mother bear, with a tiny teddy under her arm – Eddy's teddy. They quickly switch teddies and run away in different directions. A funny, fast-paced book for youngsters with strong nerves. Arresting, larger than life illustrations by the author. Look out for the mummy bear that is so big she takes up the whole page. Amusing and dramatic. **Also by this author:** *It's the Bear; Duck in the Truck*

The Farmyard Tales
by Heather Amery
illustrated by Stephen Cartwright
Usborne €6.15

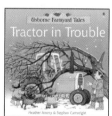

These charming and gentle tales are set on Apple Tree Farm. The text is simple and easy to follow and the illustrations are colourful and child friendly. They are ideal for sharing with young children and also make good early readers for the 4+ age group.

Madeline
by Ludwig Bemelmans
Scholastic €12.30

'In an old house in Paris that was covered in vines, lived twelve little girls in two straight lines', so begins this charming 1939 picture book which still enchants children today. Its striking, stylised illustrations are still as fresh and original as they were in the 1930s. An engaging book that's a little different.

The Runaway Train
by Benedict Blathwayt
Red Fox €7.70

The illustrations in this book are meticulously detailed and made to pore over. On one page you can see horses being led back to their stables, two young lovers, tourists visiting a ruined abbey and a vast array of interlinking roads, railway lines and rivers. The story itself is beguiling, with a regular refrain for everyone to join in. But it's the illustrations which keep children coming back to this book time and time again. **Also by this author:** *The Great Big Little Red Train*

The Snowman
by Raymond Briggs
Puffin €9.25

This picture book about the friendship between a boy and a snowman has become a Christmas classic. The mystical, glowing illustrations in snowy shades of white, blue and grey, make every page sing. A lovely book to share with a child of four or over.
Also by this author: *Fungus the Bogeyman*

Handa's Surprise
by Eileen Browne
Walker Books €9.25

Handa has a surprise for her friend, Akeya. She's taking her a huge basket of fruit, balancing it on her head: a yellow banana, a round juicy orange, and a creamy green avocado. But as she walks along, the naughty animals help themselves to her kind gift. A simple story, with exotic looking and vibrantly coloured illustrations. Great fun to share with children, who love being in on the animals' tricks.
Also available in a wonderfully entertaining book and DVD edition

One Snowy Night
by Nick Butterworth
HarperCollins €9.25

A snowy delight. It's a cold and snowy night and Percy the kind hearted park-keeper gives shelter to all his woodland animal friends, with funny and dramatic consequences. This is a warm, happy kind of book, ideal for sharing with children in need of a little winter comfort. Friendly, clear, almost cartoon like illustrations which young children love.
Also by this author: *Q Pootle 5*

My Mum
by Anthony Browne Picture Corgi €9.25

A warm and funny tribute to mums by this talented author and illustrator. This mum is a fantastic cook, juggler, painter and strong woman. The illustrations are full of clever detail which will make you and your child laugh out loud. The text is simple but, combined with the witty illustrations, it works perfectly. 'Gorilla' by the same author is also excellent. A darker story, about a young girl who lives with her dad, but well worth seeking out.
Also by this author: *My Dad; My Brother*

Photograph © Penguin

All About Lauren Child

Lauren was born in 1967 and grew up in Marlborough, Wiltshire. She now lives in London. She studied art at college in Manchester and London, and worked for Damien Hirst as an assistant, before setting up her own exotic lampshade company, called 'Chandeliers for the People'.

Her first book was called *I Want a Pet* (1999) followed by the hugely popular *Clarice Bean, That's Me* (also 1999). She has won pretty much every picture book award going and there is now a BBC television programme based on her delightful Charlie and Lola books. Her distinctive use of collage and typography make her a true picture book original.

Clarice Bean, That's Me ★
by *Lauren Child* Orchard €9.25

Clarice Bean is a charming character, full of funny observations and comments. All she wants is a bit of peace from her noisy family, so when she's sent to her room in 'Big Trouble' she's only too delighted. The colourful collage illustrations are a joy to look at and to share, and the book has lots of interesting typography which will interest any older child or adult. An intelligent, funny and wry look at family life through the eyes of a young girl. It will make you laugh as much as your child.

I Am Too Absolutely Small for School
by *Lauren Child* Orchard €9.25

This book introduces the wonderful (and mostly patient) Charlie, and Lola, his little sister, who is afraid of going to school. Charlie tries to reason with her by proving how useful school will be if she needs to count elephants. The strong, clever and colourful collage illustrations will charm parents and children alike. A witty, entertaining read.

Who's Afraid of the Big Bad Book?
by *Lauren Child*
Hodder Children's Books €10.75

Reviewed by Lynn, Dubray Books, Grafton Street, Dublin

This book is a roller coaster for the imagination. Both the story and the illustrations are superb. Having fallen into a storybook, Herb meets a whole host of recognisable fairytale characters and his calamitous interactions with them result in the rewriting of a number of familiar stories. This is wonderfully funny book that both parents and children will enjoy.

Also by this author:
My Uncle is a Hunkle; I Am Not Sleepy and I Will Not Go To Bed; What Planet Are You From, Clarice Bean?; Whoops, But It Wasn't Me; I've Won, No, I've Won

Where Are You, Blue Kangaroo?
by Emma Chichester Clarke
HarperCollins €9.25

Lily is always leaving her Blue Kangaroo behind her, even though she loves him. Finally after leaving him in the zoo where he ends up being pushed into a real kangaroo's pouch, he decides he's had enough and gives her such a fright she never lets him out of her sight again. A highly original story, with stylish and elegant illustrations.
Also by this author: *Melrose and Croc Find a Smile*

Princess Smartypants
by Babette Cole
Puffin €9.25

A funny twist on the traditional princess marries prince tale. The princess knows what's what and remains happily unmarried, having fun with her pets. Witty cartoon style illustrations and hilarious text make this a read aloud winner.
Also by this author: *Prince Cinders*

Slow Loris
by Alexis Deacon
Red Fox €9.25

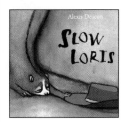

Alex Deacon is a young, award winning author/illustrator with a quirky, unusual vision. If you like picture books that are a little different and a little 'arty', this is the book for you. The story of Slow Loris, sleepy by day, party animal by night, it combines smooth, witty writing with strongly coloured, brilliantly executed illustrations. I have shared it with several children of three plus and they all love it.

Vegetable Glue
by Susan Chandler
illustrated by Elena Odriozola
Meadowside €7.70

'When my right arm fell off, I knew what to do, I stuck it back on with vegetable glue.' This is a charming, and witty book with very striking illustrations in dreamy muted colours. There's a subtle healthy eating thread running through the quirky book in verse which makes it even more 'worthy' of attention. A hidden gem which is worth seeking out.

Photographs © Macmillan

All About
Julia Donaldson and Axel Scheffler

The Gruffalo is Dubray Books' best selling picture book, and for good reason. But who are the faces behind the book?

Julia Donaldson lives in Glasgow with her husband and busking partner, Malcolm. Her first book was *A Squash and a Squeeze* (1993). She has three cats, Campsie, Gizmo and Goblin, and is very interested in wild flowers and fungi.

Axel was born in Germany in 1957 and now lives in London. His books have been translated into over twenty-nine different languages. In his spare time he likes to walk, read and make bread.

The Gruffalo was published in 1999. It has sold over two million copies to date and has already become a modern picture book classic.

The Gruffalo ★
by Julia Donaldson
illustrated by Axel Scheffler
Macmillan €9.25

Julia Donaldson's picture books are amazingly popular and this was the title that started it all. The story of a tiny, quick witted mouse and his 'invention', the horrible Gruffalo, it's great fun to read out loud. The text is repetitive, making it easy for children to join in and there are great surprises on every page. The bright, child-friendly illustrations make this a real winner.

The Smartest Giant in Town ★
by Julia Donaldson
illustrated by Axel Scheffler
Macmillan €9.25

The 'Gruffalo' team are back with another stellar picture book. George the giant is smart and kind and gives away his new clothes to the needy in his town. A charming rhyming tale about sharing, with fantastic illustrations by Axel in his characteristic colourful style. My favourite Donaldson/Scheffler title.

Also by the Donaldson/Scheffler team:
The Snail and the Whale; The Gruffalo's Child; A Squash and a Squeeze; Room on the Broom; Monkey Puzzle

Bringing Down the Moon
by Jonathan Emmett
Walker Books €9.25

A sweet, heart-warming tale about a little mole who sees the moon for the first time and decides he must have it. So he sets about trying to pull it down, much to the dismay of his animal friends. The illustrations are gently coloured and dreamy, with the night blue pages perfectly setting off the velvety fur of the small black mole.

Olivia ★
by Ian Falconer
Simon and Schuster €10.75

Olivia is a young piglet with attitude. She romps through her day, dreaming of being a ballerina, painting Pollock-like drizzle paintings on the walls, and wearing her mother out. Falconer's wry and clever text is perfectly pitched but it's his striking artwork that really steals the show. Using mainly black and white, with a dash of pillarbox red, his illustrations are dramatic and highly original.

Also by this author: *Olivia Saves the Circus*

You, Me and the Big Blue Sea
by Marie Louise Fitzpatrick
Gullane €9.25

An unusual and clever picture book set in the 1860's, by an award winning Irish author/illustrator. An observant young boy and his mother remember a voyage together but each remembers different things. In this book, the illustrations tell a different story to the text, enabling the child to get 'one up' on the parent reading it. Most empowering for them.

Also by this author: *Izzy and Skunk*

The Selfish Crocodile
by Faustin Charles
illustrated by Mike Terry
Bloomsbury €9.25

Every morning a very large and very snappy crocodile shouts this selfish message: 'Stay away from my river! It's my river! If you come in my river, I'll eat you all!' The other animals are scared and don't know what to do. But one day the selfish crocodile needs help and a clever little mouse finds a way to solve everyone's dilemma. The rainbow-bright, bold illustrations bring this witty story to life.

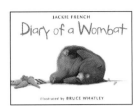

Diary of a Wombat
by Jackie French
illustrated by Bruce Whatley
HarperCollins €9.25

An Australian classic. A wombat's work is never done. There are holes to be dug and territory to be defended – and don't forget all that eating and sleeping that needs to be squeezed in too. An engaging book, featuring a cute and endearing wombat with attitude who needs her sleep. Written in diary format, the charming, comic text will make you smile. Meet the Bridget Jones of the wombat world.

Wolves
by Emily Gravett
Macmillan €9.25

Winner of the 2005 Kate Greenaway Medal. When Rabbit borrows a book about wolves from the library, a sinister animal with sharp claws and a bushy tail starts to creep right off the pages. With two surprise endings and lots of fun inserts like a 'real' library ticket, this is a real winner for all ages. The highly original, eye catching and stylish illustrations are brilliant. Not for the faint hearted parent but children find it delightfully scary and different.
Also by this author: *Monkey and Me; Little Mouse's Big Book of Fears*

Meerkat Mail
by Emily Gravett
Macmillan €9.25

Sunny is a meerkat who lives with his enormous family in the Kalahari Desert. One day he decides he needs a little space, so he packs his bags and sets off to visit his mongoose cousins. But Sunny just doesn't fit in. And who's that shadowy figure who always seems to be following him? A highly original story with brilliantly executed illustrations; watch out for Emily Gravett, she's going to be huge.

Katie Morag Delivers the Mail
by Mairi Hedderwick
Red Fox €7.70

Katie Morag lives in the post office and shop on the remote Scottish island of Struay. She's given the job of delivering five parcels to different people on the island but four of the addresses get washed away. Luckily, clever and resourceful Granny Island is there to save the day. A charming, gentle story about a close knit rural community with delightful watercolour illustrations.

Dogger ★
by Shirley Hughes
Red Fox €9.25

A boy called Dave loves his toy dog, Dogger. When Dogger goes missing, Dave is distraught but his kind sister manages to find the dog and save the day. All children and parents will feel for Dave, even if they have never had a Dogger. A sweet story with friendly and warm illustrations. Hughes has a real knack for getting her characters' expressions just right, and her grubby toddlers and tousled-haired children are a joy.

Also by this author: *Annie Rose is My Little Sister; The Big Alfie and Annie Rose Storybook*

Dear Greenpeace
by Simon James
Walker Books €7.70

Emily is worried that the whale in her pond is unhappy, so she writes to Greenpeace for advice. They gently point out that whales are better off in the ocean, but Emily is a determined little thing and so writes back to them again and again. And Emily's 'letters' are included in the book. Funny, touching, sad; everything a good book should be. With great illustrations by the author.

Also by this author: *Leon and Bob*

The Shepherd Boy
by Kim Lewis
Walker Books €7.70

Kim Lewis lives on a farm in Northumberland with her husband, two children and six border collies. This book was based on the experiences of her son's first shepherding year, when he was three. A touching and genuinely moving story with soft, realistic coloured pencil illustrations.

Also by this author: *Goodnight Harry; Floss*

The Tiger Who Came to Tea ★
by Judith Kerr
HarperCollins €9.25

One evening a huge tiger joins Sophie and her mother for tea. He eats all the food in the house and even drinks all the water from the taps, so Sophie's dad brings them out for tea. A charming and gentle tale with colourful, strong illustrations. An enduring classic.

Also by this author: *Mog, the Forgetful Cat*

Photograph © HarperCollins

All About Oliver Jeffers

Oliver was born in Western Australia in 1977 and reared in Belfast. He studied Visual Communication at the University of Ulster. In 2007 he won an Irish Book Award for his picture book for older children, *The Incredible Book Eating Boy*, and he also won the Nestlé Children's Book Award in 2005 for *Lost and Found*. He says he 'loves plastic food, suitcase handles and Elvis, and has developed a bizarre habit of endlessly writing lists he never reads.' He also remains hell bent on travelling all over the world.

How to Catch a Star ★
by *Oliver Jeffers* HarperCollins €9.25

This is Oliver Jeffer's first picture book. Winner of the Smarties Award, it tells the story of a young boy who wants to catch a star from the sky and befriend it. He tries all kinds of things from lassoing it with a life buoy, to taking to the skies in a rocket, but the answer to his problem lies on the sand in front of his feet. With eye catching watercolour illustrations in glowing colours and a charming and well written story, this book works a treat with children of three and over.

Lost and Found ★
by *Oliver Jeffers* HarperCollins €9.25

This is one of my favourite picture books of all time. The story is charming, the illustrations exceptional, but it's the truth behind the words that really gets me every time I read it. When a penguin turns up on a young boy's doorstep, the boy decides to bring him home to the South Pole. They make the daring sea voyage in a small rowing boat but it's only when the boy rows away that he realises the penguin wasn't lost at all, he was just lonely. Jeffer's illustrations glow and the final spread, of the rowing boat floating on an azure sea above a family of whales is blissful. Don't miss it.

The Incredible Book Eating Boy ★
by *Oliver Jeffers* HarperCollins €9.25

Henry loves books so much, he literally eats them up. Soon he's smarter than his teacher, but his unorthodox diet begins to cause him digestive and mental problems. Jeffers' illustrations are astounding, lifting mixed media to another level. His images are painstakingly painted on pages or covers of old books and dog-eared graph paper, and the text is lovingly hand written or typed using an old fashioned typewriter and then carefully manipulated. Age four and over.
Also by this author: *The Way Back Home*

Little Beaver and the Echo
by Amy MacDonald
illustrated by Sarah Fox-Davies
Walker Books €9.25

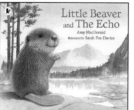 Little Beaver is lonely and goes in search of the echo across the lake. On his journey, he makes some new friends and finds that to have friends you have to be a friend first. The gentle, well written text makes this a great read aloud book at bedtime. The illustrations are realistic and beautifully coloured. A good choice for young nature lovers.
Also available in a book and DVD edition.

Elmer the Patchwork Elephant
by David McKee
Red Fox €9.25

 Elmer loves playing tricks on his friends. One day he decides to go grey, like all the other elephants, with hilarious consequences. The funny, thoughtful story and bright, eye catching illustrations make this picture book a real favourite.

Five Minutes' Peace
by Jill Murphy
Walker Books €9.25

 All Mrs Large, the elephant, wants is a few minutes' peace from her lively children. But her little elephant children have other ideas. This is a book that both parents and children will relate to! A fun bedtime read with strong, colourful illustrations.

Captain Adbul's Pirate School
by Colin McNaughton
Walker Books €9.25

 Children love pirates, and this lively book is the diary of a reluctant pirate pupil, Pickles. She hates the Captain's terrible teaching – how to make cannon balls, how to swear like a pirate, and the right way to say 'ooh arrgh!' – so she leads a mutiny and has a great life robbing other pirates. Great fun, with cracking illustrations; a romp of a book. Also great with older children of six plus.

The Happy Prince
by Jane Ray (adapted from the story by Oscar Wilde)
Orchard Books €9.25

The Happy Prince is a wonderful story, tragic and moving, and it deserves to be better known. A golden statue sees all the misery of a city from his high perch. He asks his swallow friend to pick off his gold leaf and give it to the poor. It's a fairy tale that can be enjoyed by all ages and the glittering illustrations by Jane Ray bring it to life. A classic.
Also by this illustrator: *A Balloon for Grandad*

What Do People Do All Day?
by Richard Scarry
HarperCollins €9.25

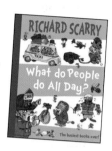

I adored Richard Scarry as a child, still do, and was delighted to see some of his books back in print. This is one of my all time favourites. It's packed with things to spot on every page, as it introduces the world of work to children in a fun way – from dressmakers and mothers to sailors and builders. No children's booksellers I'm afraid, but pretty much everything else. Great fun to share with a child.
Also by this author: *Cars, Trucks and Things That Go*

Where the Wild Things Are ☆
by Maurice Sendak
HarperCollins €9.25

This picture book first came out in the 1960s and has remained a bestseller ever since. The story of Max, a young boy who is sent to bed for terrorising the dog with a fork and finds himself King in a strange, fantasy world, this book has striking, unusual artwork and lyrical text. For children who like being a little scared, and parents who like books with a little 'bite'. A wonderful, wonderful book. I can't recommend it highly enough. And don't be afraid of the monsters; he based them on his maiden aunts.

Faster, Faster, Nice and Slow
by Nick Sharratt and Sue Heap
Puffin €9.25

A fun and useful book about opposites. Sue and Nick are best friends in real life and the books they write and illustrate together are full of energy and wit. Sue's painterly work contrasts delightfully with Nick's more stylised illustrations, and even the youngest child can have fun spotting and talking about the different methods of creating a picture.

Come On, Daisy!
by Jane Simmonds
Orchard Books €9.25

'You must stay close, Daisy,' says Mama Duck. But Daisy doesn't listen, which leads to all kinds of trouble. Short, simple text combined with brightly coloured, sunny illustrations make this a perfect book for toddlers and younger children. There's a useful lesson there for young wanderers too.

Winnie the Witch
by Valerie Thomas
illustrated by Korky Paul
Oxford University Press €12.30

Winner of the Children's Book Award, this picture book is great fun. Winnie the Witch has had enough of her cat, Wilbur, who keeps tripping her up, so she decides to turn him green. But poor Wilbur isn't happy with this at all. A witty book which promotes tolerance among friends. The illustrations by Korky Paul are unusual and eye catching – Winnie is a triumph of quirky witchiness.
Also by this author: *Winnie's Midnight Dragon*

Three Little Wolves and the Big Bad Pig
by Eugene Trivizas
illustrated by Helen Oxenbury
Egmont Books €9.25

A clever retelling of the classic fairy story. In this version the pig is the baddie and the wolves must outwit him with their increasingly elaborate houses, made from concrete, plexi-glass and finally sweet-scented flowers. The illustrations by Helen Oxenbury are highly detailed, beautifully coloured and witty.

Eloise
by Kay Thompson
illustrated by Hilary Knight
Simon and Schuster €10.75

If I'm having a bad day, Eloise never fails to make me laugh. In fact, she's loved by girls of all ages, from four to ninety-four. Eloise is an eccentric six-year-old who lives with her long suffering nanny at The Plaza Hotel in New York. Her parents are ultra rich and largely leave her to her own devices, with hilarious consequences. Divine illustrations too. Perfect for a knowing five-year-old and equally fun for her mother.

Photograph © Walker Books

All About Martin Wadell

Martin Waddell, born in 1941, works in an old stone barn beside his house in Newcastle, Co. Down. He has three grown-up sons.

TEN THINGS YOU DIDN'T KNOW ABOUT MARTIN WADDELL

1. I can wiggle my ears.
2. I am a very noisy tennis player.
3. I had a cat that could open doors.
4. My dog hears my stories before I write them.
5. I scored a hat trick on my debut in adult football, but wound up as a goalkeeper.
6. I used to run a junk stall.
7. I like bringing up egg-shaped stones from the beach to my garden.
8. I like apple tarts.
9. I hate onions.
10. I'm a happy man.

Can't You Sleep, Little Bear
by Martin Waddell
illustrated by Barbara Firth
Walker Books €9.25

Little Bear is afraid of the dark and can't sleep. But Big Bear finds a clever way of reassuring him. He brings him outside and shows him the moon and the stars. This story has been a favourite for many years and still charms to this day. The illustrations by Barbara Firth are adorable; her bears are comfortingly solid and weighty. If your child is prone to 'amateur dramatics' and is *not* afraid of the dark, better give this one a miss.
Also by this author: *A Kitten Called Moonlight*

SOME MORE OF OUR FAVOURITES:

I Want to Be
by Tony Ross

Vote for Duck
by Doreen Cronin

There's No Such Thing as a Ghostie
by Cressida Cowell

Mrs McTats and her Houseful of Cats
by Alyssa Satin Capucilli and Joan Rankin

The Kipper Books
by Mick Inkpen

Six Dinner Sid
by Inga Moore

The Paper Bag Princess
by Robert Munsch

The Lighthouse Keeper's Breakfast
by Ronda and David Armitage

Ten in the Bed
by Penny Dale

Kiss Good Night, Sam
by Amy Hest

How Do Dinosaurs Say Goodnight?
by Jane Yolen

Harry and the Dinosaurs Go Wild
by Ian Whybrow

Pants
by Giles Andreae and Nick Sharratt

Mister Magnolia
by Quentin Blake

Mr Gumpy's Outing
by John Burningham

Frog in Love
by Max Velthuijs

The Whale's Song
by Dyan Sheldon

Sheep in Wolves Clothing
by Satoshi Kitamura

Egg
by M P Robertson

Dali and the Path of Dreams
by Anna Obiols

Don't Let the Pigeon Drive the Bus
by Mo Williams

FAIRY TALE COLLECTIONS

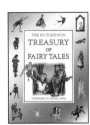

The Hutchinson Treasury of Fairy Tales
Various authors and illustrators
Hutchinson €30.75

This handsome book brings together all the old favourites from 'Cinderella' to 'Little Red Riding Hood'. It also includes Oscar Wilde's 'The Selfish Giant' and Andersen's haunting 'The Snow Queen'. All illustrated by top artists from Quentin Blake to Shirley Hughes. A marvellous book for any child's library. Age four and over.

The Usborne Book of Fairy Tales
by Heather Amery
illustrated by Stephen Cartwright
Usborne €10.75

A useful, fun introduction to fairy tales for younger children. Six tales are included in this book: Cinderella, Rumpelstiltskin, Little Red Riding Hood, Sleeping Beauty, Goldilocks and the Three Bears, and The Three Little Pigs. There is dual-level text on each page, with a simple line for a child to read and a more complex one for an adult or older child. Bright, cartoon like illustrations. Age three and over.

The Oxford Treasury of Fairy Tales
by Geraldine McCaughrean
illustrated by Sophy Williams
Oxford University Press €15.40

The classic fairy tales, retold by award winning children's author, Geraldine McCaughrean. From Sleeping Beauty, to Snow White, Cinderella, and The Princess and the Pea, all the old favourites are here, along with a few more unusual tales like Cap-of-Rushes and The Tinderbox. The delicate and atmospheric illustrations by Sophy Williams set off the tales beautifully. A great book to share with older children of five plus.

The Fairy Tales
Translated by David Walser
illustrated by Jan Pienkowski
Puffin €23.10

If you like your fairy tales with real bite, this is the collection for you. Freshly translated from the originals by David Walser, this includes the more grisly ending for Cinderella's step mother (dancing in red-hot iron shoes). Not for the squeamish but it didn't seem to bother my four-year-old. The silhouette illustrations by Pienkowski are arresting and stunningly beautiful. In our technicolour world, they look modern yet timeless, a treat for the eye.

Also recommended:
Fairy Tales by Berlie Doherty, **illustrated by Jane Ray**

GIFT BOOKS AND CLASSICS TO READ ALOUD

The Hutchinson Treasury of Children's Literature
Various authors and illustrators
Hutchinson €30.75

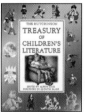

A lovely hardback collection of picture books, stories, poems and book extracts for children from birth to ten. Includes the complete *Alfie's Feet* by Shirley Hughes, *Mr Gumpy's Outing* by John Burningham, and many other picture books. Each page is illustrated by one of a host of talented and well-known illustrators, from Quentin Blake to Angela Barrett and Tony Ross. A book to keep and treasure for years. Age three and over.

The Shirley Hughes Collection
Bodley Head €30.75

Author and illustrator, Shirley Hughes was awarded an OBE for her lifetime's work. All the Hughes favourites are collected together in this handsome book, from the charming 'Alfie' series, to the all time favourite, *Dogger*.

The Roald Dahl Treasury
Puffin €20.00

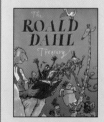

Roald Dahl is a must for any child's library and excerpts from all his best books are gathered together in this hardback volume, along with poems, letters, and short stories. Illustrated by the magical Quentin Blake.

Winnie the Pooh
by A A Milne
illustrated by E H Shepard
Egmont €20.00

No child should grow up without the wisdom of Pooh to guide them. Ideal for reading aloud, the Pooh stories have charmed generations of children. Illustrated with wonderfully exuberant line drawings by the original illustrator, E H Shepard.

Beatrix Potter Complete Tales
Warne €46.15

This charming cloth bound book brings together Potter's best loved tales, from Peter Rabbit to Tom Kitten. An extremely handsome book, one to be kept and savoured.

There are many other Potter collections available; ask your local Dubray Books children's buyer for details.

NOVELTY AND POP-UP BOOKS

The Jolly Postman
by Janet and Allan Ahlberg Viking €20.00

One of the most innovative books for younger children. The Jolly Postman delivers his letters to a host of fairy tale characters. Goldilocks sends a 'sorry' letter to the Three Bears, and the Big Bad Wolf is issued a writ on behalf of both Red Riding Hood and the Three Little Pigs. Each piece of post comes in its own special envelope, making it a truly interactive book. Hilarious stuff, brilliantly illustrated. A novelty book classic. Age 4+

Also by this author/illustrator combo: *The Jolly Christmas Postman*

The Haunted House
by Jan Pienkowski
Walker Books €20.00

Nearly thirty years after it was first published, this book is still delighting children and making them squeal. In the haunted house, nothing is as it seems. As you open every page, a new spine-tingling surprise is in store. Clever paper engineering combined with knock out illustrations make this one of the most fun books around. Perfect for little horrors of three plus who like to be scared. Winner of the Kate Greenaway Medal in 1979.

The Wonderful Wizard of Oz
by Robert Sabuda
Simon and Schuster €30.75

Sabuda really is a master craftsman and his pop-up books amaze and delight both children and adults. This is one of my favourites. The magical story lends itself to incredible pop up scenes, from the house flying through the air to the glowing Emerald city. This book even comes with its own pair of emerald glasses.

Also by this author: *Alice's Adventures in Wonderland; The Night Before Christmas*

The Wheels on the Bus
by Paul Zelinsky
Orchard Books €20.00

This favourite children's song is illustrated in zany colour by Paul Zelinsky. Each page features lots of moving parts and pop-ups, ideal for making the reading experience fun for younger children, and parents will enjoy the strong, graphic illustrations too. A book and a toy all in one. The wheels on the bus really do go round and round in this book!

Also recommended:
The Great Grammar Book
by Kate Petty

Introduction

Most children will learn to read between the ages of five and eight. For some lucky children this comes quickly and easily, for others it takes more time and is much more difficult. The most important thing is that they continue to enjoy books and stories. It's vital to keep reading to them, even when they have grasped the mechanics of reading. It's also important to allow them revisit their favourite old picture books, even if you think they should have grown out of them.

If you are worried about your child's reading, do talk to their teacher and get some advice. But rest assured that a child who doesn't take to reading quickly or easily will often become a voracious reader once it all starts to click into place. I know, as I didn't start reading fluently until I was nine and now I'd read all day if I could. My parents were very worried about me, but they never stopped reading aloud. It made all the difference.

> You may have riches and wealth untold,
> With baskets of jewels and caskets of gold.
> But richer than I you will never be,
> For I had a mother who read to me.
>
> – Strickland W Gillilan (1936)

Here's what to look out for in a book for a young reader of Age 5 to 9:

- For children who are starting to read look for short chapters, limited vocabulary and a picture on every page to help them to decode the meaning of the words.
- Look for uncluttered pages with clearly printed text that is easy to make out with the eye.
- Match the book to your child's tastes and interests – continue to keep the whole reading experience fun.
- Don't forget picture books when they can read – there are some great picture books for older readers. Your child's visual literacy is important too – the way in which they can 'read' a picture and make out what is happening is a vital skill, often overlooked.
- Funny, slightly rude books, like those by Eoin Colfer and Roddy Doyle, are good for reluctant readers (who tend to be boys) – these are marked 'Reluctant Reader' in the reviews.

A Note on Reading Aloud

Children can listen to books that might be too difficult for them to tackle for themselves. Charlotte's Web makes an excellent read aloud, as does Tom's Midnight Garden. Check out the Age 8 to 12 Years section for more ideas. It's also a great way to introduce the classics to children, books like Swallows and Amazons and Black Beauty. Books on tape also make great bedtime listening, but nothing can beat being read to. Don't think because a child can now read fluently that you can stop. Continue for as long as you are both enjoying it and look out for the titles marked 'Read Aloud' in the reviews following.

Puffin and Macmillan publish some great age-ranged story collections which are ideal for reading aloud. Some of my favourite books on tape (or CD) which can be enjoyed by the whole family include the Roald Dahl stories (Puffin Audio Books), and Winnie the Pooh read by Alan Bennett (BBC Radio Collection).

PICTURE BOOKS AGE 5+

Mummy Laid an Egg
by Babette Cole Red Fox €9.25

Mum and Dad tell their children all about the birds and the bees but they get it all wrong. So it's up to the children to set them right. A laugh a minute guide to the real facts of life, with hilarious cartoon illustrations by the author. A great book for sharing with your children, and for dealing with the facts of life in a light-hearted, humorous way.

The Princess and the Pea
by Lauren Child
Puffin €10.75

A sumptuous picture book and a dream of a book for a 'girly-girl'. Each page of this book features small 3-D sets hand crafted by Child and 'captured' by photographer Polly Borland. The text of this rewritten classic is perfectly pitched for reading aloud to a knowing four or five-year-old, and, with its traditional fairy tale girl meets boy storyline (with a slight twist), it will also appeal to older children.

The Stinky Cheese Man
by John Scieszka
illustrated by Lane Smith
Puffin €10.75

An irreverent take on traditional fairy stories. Goldilocks and the Three Elephants and Little Red Running Shorts tell their twisted tales in this fresh, unusual book. The illustrations by Lane Smith are dramatic and stylised, ideal for older children; she uses collage, unusual images and creative typography to produce her highly original pictures.
Also by this author: *The True Story of the Three Little Pigs*

How to Live Forever
by Colin Thompson
Red Fox €9.25

Peter and his family live among the Quinces in the cookery section of a magical and mystical library. At night, when the library comes to life, Peter ventures out of his home to find a missing book, 'How To Live Forever' and to learn the secrets between its pages. Highly detailed illustrations, combined with an interesting plot which deals in an original way with life and death, make this a good choice for older children.

Also recommended:
Weslandia by Paul Fleischman, illustrated by Kevin Hawkes

VERY FIRST READERS: AGE 5 TO 7 YEARS

Children learn to read at different ages. For some it's five, for others it's seven or eight. Don't worry if your child doesn't pick it up quickly, some are slow burners. Just read to them, share books with them and give it time. Try not to make reading a chore for either you or your child. It's vitally important at this stage that they don't start to associate books with hard work. Again, if you're worried, ask your child's teacher for help and advice.

There are lots of books specially designed for children who are just starting to read. Books in a series have a consistent level of vocabulary and language. A good reading series makes reading fun and combines easy to read text with lively, child friendly illustrations. Here are some of our favourites:

Dr Seuss Beginner Books

The Dr Seuss books are still as popular as ever. With zany rhymes and a host of colourful, whacky characters, these rhyming tales are just right for imaginative children to start reading for themselves.

Happy Families

A great series of books that cleverly bridges the gap between picture books and chapter books. Written by Allan Ahlberg and illustrated by a variety of top illustrators from Janet Ahlberg to Colin McNaughton, they are funny, smart and colourful.

Mrs Wobble the Waitress
by Allan Ahlberg
illustrated by Janet Ahlberg
Puffin €6.15

Mrs Wobble and her family set up a new restaurant with hilarious consequences.

O'BRIEN PRESS PANDA SERIES

The Panda Series by Irish publisher, O'Brien Press, has been a huge success. There are now over thirty in the series and there's something for every child, from gentle animal stories to funny tales of bold Horrid Henry-like boys. The books are carefully designed with clear, bright covers and child friendly black and white illustrations.

For older readers of six plus, the Flyers Series, again from O'Brien Press, is ideal. The books in this series have short chapters and longer sentences, including three titles from the brilliant Eoin Colfer, author of the Artemis Fowl books.

There are many other reading series from the various publishers, but the Bananas, published by Egmont, stand out. They have a policy of using only the best authors and illustrators, from Julia Donaldson to Jacqueline Wilson. There are four different stages: Green Bananas for the youngest readers, followed by Blue, Red and Yellow Bananas.

Granny's Teeth (Panda Series)
by Brianog Brady Dawson
illustrated by Michael Connor
O'Brien Press €5.95

Danny is the kind of boy who is always in trouble, so when Granny's teeth go missing guess where they turn up? A great choice for any child who likes a good laugh.

Going Potty (Flyers Series)
by Eoin Colfer
illustrated by Woody
O'Brien Press €5.95

Ed Cooper is a senior infant now and that means using the big boys' toilet. Ed needs 'to go' but he's too scared. He can't hold on forever, but maybe, just maybe, there's a way out – his special potty. Gran's potty is no ordinary potty but can it help save the day? Brilliantly funny story with cartoon-style black and white illustrations. A real winner.

Larkspur and the Grand March
by Mary Arrigan
illustrated by Debbie Boon
Egmont €6.15

A funny, charming story in the Red Banana range for 'improving readers' (the next step after beginners) by a highly talented Irish writer. Larkspur is a lion with a difference; he can sing opera.

A WORD ON SERIES BOOKS: AGE 6 TO 9

The great thing about books in a series is that they keep children reading. As parents, we sometimes worry that our children are only reading one kind of book but rest assured, once they catch the reading bug, they will move on to other books. I was an avid and passionate Enid Blyton and Nancy Drew fan in my day.

Try reading aloud from other books to give them a more rounded reading experience. We have suggested some good books to read aloud in the reviews on pages 36 to 47, marked 'Read Aloud' after the title. And don't forget picture books, they're not just for younger children. Finally, books for more reluctant readers are marked 'Reluctant Readers' after the title.

Some of our favourite series books for emerging readers are:
(Other individual titles are reviewed on pages 36 to 47)

Magic Kitten Series
by Sue Bentley
Puffin €6.15

My Secret Unicorn Series
by Linda Chapman
Puffin €7.70

Animal Ark Pets Series
by Lucy Daniels
Hodder €6.15

The Rainbow Fairies Series
by Daisy Meadows
Orchard €6.15

Witch in Training Series
by Maeve Friel
HarperCollins €6.15

My Magical Pony Series
by Jenny Oldfield
Hodder €7.70

Mermaid SOS Series
by Gillian Shields
Bloomsbury €6.15

Felicity Wishes Series
by Emma Thomson
Hodder €6.15

Harry the Poisonous Centipede
by Lynne Reid Banks
HarperCollins €7.70

Billed as 'a story to make you squirm' this is a very funny tale for younger readers. Harry is not very brave. He likes to eat things that wriggle and crackle, and things that are juicy and munchy. But there are some things that even a poisonous centipede shouldn't try to eat – dangerous things like Hoo-Mins. Accompanied by his friend, George, Harry goes on some deliciously edible adventures. Great illustrations by Tony Ross.

The Secret Seven Series
by Enid Blyton
Hodder €6.15

No child should grow up without a good taste of the Blyton magic. Yes, they are a little dated now, but they still charm and entertain children and their adult 'read-alouders'. The Secret Seven is the perfect introduction to adventure stories for young readers. And they can move on to the Famous Five next.

A Bear Called Paddington
(Read Aloud)
by Michael Bond
HarperCollins €7.70

Paddington is still a great favourite with children and makes a great read aloud bedtime story. When the Brown family find a bear at Paddington Station, they have no idea how much trouble this marmalade lover will get them into. Sweet, charming and laugh out loud funny.
Also by this author: *Olga da Polga*

Flat Stanley
by Jeff Brown
Mammoth €9.25

Reviewed by Amanda, Dubray Books, Blackrock

When Stanley wakes up one morning, his brother is yelling. A bulletin board fell on Stanley during the night and now he is only half an inch thick. He cheerfully makes the most of his new shape, gets posted to California for a free holiday, foils an art gallery robbery and retrieves a lost ring. But soon he longs to be the right size again. A touching book about size – and children do worry about their size – with distinctive line drawings by Tomi Unger. Delightfully funny.
Also by this author: *Invisible Stanley*

Dear Me
by Marie Burlington
O'Brien Press €6.95

While Cathy's mum is in hospital, she goes to stay with her grandfather for the summer. Written in the form of a diary, this is a well written, charming book which deals with depression, family problems and loneliness in a sensitive way. Cathy is a brave and resourceful girl and the reader follows her journey with interest. Highly recommended for any Jacqueline Wilson fans.

The Big Cup Collection
by Rob Childs
Young Corgi €7.70

Rob Childs was a teacher and these books are perfectly pitched to a young (and mainly male) audience. They are full of action and drama and would suit any football fan of six plus. Set in Danebridge School, pupils Andrew and Chris Weston both play on the football team. Meet them and their football friends in these fast paced and fun books.

Ed's Bed (Reluctant Readers)
by Eoin Colfer
O'Brien Press €5.95

A witty, well written book about bed wetting. Ed Cooper is having problems in school: he just can't get his head around his times tables. Then poor Ed starts wetting the bed too. A happy ending comes courtesy of his mum and dad's clever rescue plan. Colfer is perfectly in tune with young children and their very real concerns and this book manages to be both reassuring and very, very funny.
Also by this author: *The Legend of Spud Murphy; The Worst Boy in the World*

Utterly Me, Clarice Bean (Read Aloud)
by Lauren Child Orchard €9.25

Clarice Bean is what my mother would call 'a hoot'. Her eccentric family are brilliantly drawn, the mum spends her life 'gribbling' about pants on the floor, and her brother Minal is 'utterly a nuisance' with his stupid jokes. Clarice has to do a 'dreary' book project, and chooses to write about her hero, Ruby Redford, an eleven-year-old detective, with hilarious results. Child is known for her typographic razzmatazz and she puts it to excellent use in Clarice's breathless diary.
Also by this author: *Clarice Bean Spells Trouble; Don't Look Now, Clarice Bean*

Elephant at the Door
by Don Conroy Poolbeg Press €5.07

Don Conroy is a writer, environmentalist and artist who lives in Dublin. Well know for his Den TV art slots, his books for young readers combine his child-like joie de vivre with his love of nature, to great effect. In this book a child wishes for an elephant and gets an awful fright when one appears at the front door. A very funny, sweet book about being careful what you wish for.
Also by this author: *The Bookworm Who Turned Over a New Leaf*

The Tree House (Read Aloud)
by Gillian Cross
Oxford University Press €7.70

This book is a little gem. Gently, carefully written with a clever twist at the end, it has been one of my favourite read alouds for many years now and it's also perfect for younger readers to tackle alone. William and Sprog ask their dad to build them a tree house but then he has to go abroad to work. Every month, he sends them home a very special present. Deceptively simple, this short book packs a real emotional punch.

Fantastic Mr Fox (Read Aloud) ★
by Roald Dahl
illustrated by Quentin Blake
Puffin €7.70

This is my favourite Roald Dahl book of all time. Chicken farmers Boggins, Bunce and Bean ('One fat, one short, one lean') are determined to catch Mr Fox. He's too clever for them by half and outwits them at every turn. A brilliantly funny book, ideal for reading aloud, it never fails to make me laugh. The wonderfully lively line drawings by Quentin Blake add to its brilliance. Simple yet pure genius. Don't miss it!

The Giraffe and Pelly and Me (Read Aloud)
by Roald Dahl
illustrated by Quentin Blake
Puffin €7.70

This is the compelling tale of the Ladderless Window Cleaning Company, featuring the giraffe as ladder, the pelican as bucket and the monkey as cleaner, along with their friend Billy. When the company embark on the biggest job of their lives, cleaning all 677 windows of the Duke of Hampshire's house, no one can predict the consequences. Hilarious stuff.
Also by this author: *The Twits; The Magic Finger*

Princess Mirror-Belle
by Julia Donaldson
Macmillan €6.15

Julia Donaldson is best known for her picture books but this is a lovely, fun princess story for young readers. Ellen gets a shock when her double, Mirror-Belle, steps out of the bathroom mirror. She's a princess all right, but a very mischievous one who gets Ellen in all kinds of trouble. A simple yet clever story which will have your child hooting with laughter. Look out for the other Princess Mirror-Belle stories too. **Also by this author:** *The Giants and the Joneses; Princess Mirror-Belle and the Flying Horse*

The Giggler Treatment (Reluctant Readers)
by Roddy Doyle
Scholastic €7.70

Reviewed by Aisling,
Dubray Books, Grafton Street, Dublin

This book is laugh out loud funny from start to finish. Whenever an adult is mean or unfair to a child, the Gigglers set up dog poo traps for the adults to walk into. The whole story happens in a matter of minutes, switching between each character's hilarious point of view. Roddy Doyle's humour is delightfully rude and will appeal to any child aged 6 to 10. **Also by this author:** *Rover Saves Christmas; The Meanwhile Adventures; Wilderness (Older readers of twelve plus)*

Bill's New Frock
by Anne Fine
Egmont €7.70

This is a brilliantly funny and rather subversive book about a boy called Bill. One morning he wakes up to find he's turned into a girl overnight and has to wear a silly pink dress to school. He has to live his day as a girl, a strange new experience for him. Highly original and very clever. All boys of a certain age should be made read it, and their dads too. Anne Fine is a great writer for younger children; do seek her out. **Also by this author:** *How to Write Really Badly*

My Naughty Little Sister (Read Aloud)
by Dorothy Edwards, illustrated by Shirley Hughes
Egmont €6.15

First published in 1952, these warm and nostalgic stories still strike a chord with modern children. They were originally written for the BBC's Listen with Mother radio programme and were based on Dorothy's recollections of her childhood and her real naughty little sister. There are several short stories in this book, making it ideal read aloud material.

The Runner
by Keith Gray
Corgi €6.15

Jason is fed up with his parents' arguments and runs away on the train to Liverpool to stay with his brother. At the station, he meets 'Jam' and decides to go on the run with him. After all, he's been let down by everyone. However Jam isn't quite all he appears, and maybe running away isn't the answer. A skilfully told story with real insight. Great black and white illustrations. Something a little gritty and a little different.

Penny the Pencil
by Eileen O'Hely
Mercier €8.99

Reviewed by Aisling, Dubray Books, Grafton Street, Dublin

Penny is a kind, friendly pencil. She loves to help her new owner with his spelling tests but is also experiencing some bullying in her new pencil case home. Soon Penny is on an adventure down the back of the sofa and in a workman's pocket. This is a fun read for children of 6 to 10. The story is playful and inventive and will keep you laughing until the end. It was nominated for the Bisto Award in 2006.

Also by this author: *Penny Goes Undercover*

Katie: The Revolting Wedding
by Mary Hooper
Bloomsbury €7.70

Katie has promised to be on her best behaviour at the wedding but, when she tumbles head first into the wedding cake, she has to find a way out of the sticky mess and fast. Katie is a charming character and this book is well written and great fun. There are several other books in the Katie series, from The Revolting Bridesmaid, to the Revolting Baby. Good fun for any young Judy Moody or Clarice Bean fans.

The Hodgeheg
by Dick King-Smith
Puffin €7.70

This book emphasises in a witty and clever way the importance of road safety. Max is a rather ordinary little hedgehog until one day he becomes the hedgehog pioneer of road safety, spurred on by his Aunt Betty's tragic death. Lots of surprises are in store for the reader and Max is a sweet, brave little fellow who becomes a hedgehog hero. A delightful book for younger readers.

Also by this author: *The Sheep Pig; The School Mouse*

The Sophie Stories (Read Aloud) *
by Dick King-Smith
Walker Books €7.70

Sophie is a wonderful character, a resourceful four-year-old who has ambitions to become a 'lady farmer'. In the stories we are introduced to a host of Sophie's relations and animal friends in a charming, realistic manner. This is a well written and entertaining series, ideally suited for young girls who know their own minds. I adore Sophie's reluctant fiancé and his efforts to escape Sophie's determined planning. The gentle line drawings by David Parkins enhance the stories. **Also by this author:** *Harry's Mad; The Queen's Nose*

Ruby Rogers: Get a Life
by Sue Limb
Bloomsbury €7.70

Ruby's teacher asks her to help look after a new girl in school called Lauren Tucker. Soon Lauren has upset the uneasy equilibrium between Ruby and her best friend, Yasmin. Meanwhile, Ruby's brother has a new girlfriend and Ruby is not sure whether she likes her or not. St Valentine's Day is just around the corner, time for some devilment. Friendship is examined in a witty and touching manner in this well written book. Another good choice for Clarice Bean or Judy Moody fans. **Also by this author:** *Ruby Rogers is a Waste of Space*

Judy Moody: Around the World in 8½ Days *
by Megan McDonald
Walker Books €7.70

This is the seventh book in the bestselling Judy Moody series. Judy has a 'double' in the form of Amy Namey, a member of the 'way cool' My Name is a Poem Club. While Judy is supposed to be doing her 'Around the World' class project, she's thinking about Amy instead, and her friends are starting to feel left out. Judy Moody is a brilliant creation, and her trials and adventures make hilarious reading. Also great fun to read aloud. **Also by this author:** *Judy Moody Saves the World*

Pippi Longstocking (Read Aloud)
by Astrid Lindgren Oxford University Press €23.10

Oh, I do love Pippi Longstocking. Everything is fun when she's around and her crazy adventures make great reading. Pippi is nine and lives by herself in Villekulla Cottage with a horse and a pet monkey, which means she can do exactly as she chooses. She's immensely strong, full of energy and she doesn't like rules. Wonderfully quirky and great fun to read aloud. Now available in a stunning new gift edition, illustrated by Lauren Child. **Also by this author:** *Lotta Says 'No!'*

Stink: The Incredible Shrinking Kid (Reluctant Readers)
by Megan McDonald
Walker Books €6.15

Stink is Judy Moody's younger brother, and makes perfect reading for boys as well as girls. He's always been short but now he's shrinking. So he decides to take action and tries to make himself look taller by gelling his hair up. Soon he realises that maybe being short isn't all that bad and he'll just have to wait till he's older to be tall. A funny book, featuring inventive comic strips, perfect for reluctant readers.

Charlie and the Cat Flap
by Hilary McKay
Scholastic €6.15

Charlie is a young boy who's always getting into trouble. He plans a sleepover with his friend Henry, and they've made an agreement: no itching powder, no dead flies, no super soakers. However all doesn't go as planned. If your child likes Horrid Henry or Danny from the Panda books, they'll love Charlie. Hilary McKay is an award winning author and these books sing with humour and spirit.

Evil Hairdo
by Oisín McGann
O'Brien Press €6.95

'It started with my favourite girl band, WitchCraft. They were beautiful. They could sing and dance and above all they were cool. And I wanted the WitchCraft hairdo more than anything else in the world. But then I got it, and that's when the trouble started. Because it turned out that my hair was evil.' A clever and funny story about Melanie and the mysterious and evil hairdo which tries to destroy her life. McGann's witty illustrations are great fun too. Part of the 'Forbidden Files' series for readers who like books with a spooky edge.

Also by this author: *Mad Grandad and the Mutant River; The Poison Factory*

Illustration from *Mad Grandad and the Mutant River*
© Oisín McGann, with thanks to O'Brien Press

All About Oisín McGann

Oisín McGann was born in 1973 and studied art in college. He worked in advertising in London before returning to Ireland, as he 'began to fear for his immortal soul.' He now writes and illustrates full time.

5 THINGS YOU DIDN'T KNOW ABOUT OISÍN McGANN

1. The first thing I ever published was a comic called 'Twisted'.

2. My favourite pastime is walking in the mountains.

3. I have a little bald patch on the back of my head because of a birthmark.

4. I got an A grade for Art in my Inter Cert (the old Junior Cert) without ever having done a class – there was no theory or art history in the exam back then, you just had to draw.

5. I often eat up to four or five apples a day – including the cores.

All About Joe O'Brien

When he's not writing, Joe O'Brien is an award-winning gardener. He lives in Ballyfermot in Dublin.

5 THINGS YOU DIDN'T KNOW ABOUT JOE O'BRIEN

1. I loved banana, cucumber and cheese sandwiches when I was a teenager.

2. I can wiggle my ears.

3. My favourite author of all time is Beatrix Potter.

4. My must-have plant in a garden is Lavender.

5. My biggest and most special achievement in life was becoming a father.

The Butterfly Lion ★ (Read Aloud)
by Michael Morpurgo
HarperCollins €7.70

Another fantastic book to read aloud, Morpurgo really knows how to create memorable stories. This book is about a young boy, Bertie, growing up in Africa and his lifelong friendship with a white lion. The boy is sent to boarding school in England and has to leave his animal friend behind but the butterfly lion ensures their friendship will never be forgotten. A lyrical and very moving story, beautifully written. Inspired by the author's chance meeting in a lift with Virginia McKenna of *Born Free* fame.

The Worst Witch ★ (Read Aloud)
by Jill Murphy
Puffin €7.70

Mildred Hubble is the worst student at Miss Cackle's Academy and is always getting in trouble. In this compelling story her good humour and resourcefulness save the school from disaster. A very funny, deservedly popular book, the first in a series. Each book is well written and laugh out loud funny. With their short chapters and lively prose, these books are ideal for reading aloud but also make great 'readalones'. Striking black and white illustrations throughout by the author.

Alfie Green and a Sink Full of Frogs (Reluctant Readers)
by Joe O'Brien O'Brien Press €7.95

Alfie is mad about his garden and, when frogs start to invade, he calls on his magic book for help. There are fun cartoon style black and white illustrations on every page. This is a charming tale full of gentle humour and perfectly pitched for even the most reluctant reader of six plus. Joe is a gardener and his books are informed by his work.
Also by this author: *Alfie Green and the Monkey Puzzler; Alfie Green and The Fly-Trapper*

Animals Don't Have Ghosts
by Siobhán Parkinson
O'Brien Press €6.50

Michelle's country cousins, Dara and Sinead, are visiting 'the big smoke' and Michelle delights in showing off her cosmopolitan ways. They visit the Natural History Museum, St Stephen's Green and, best of all, a shopping centre with escalators. This is a charming and very funny version of the town mouse, country mouse tale. The writing is excellent and the dialogue between the cousins crackles with wit and energy. Siobhán is one of Ireland's best and most versatile children's writers. An excellent book for children starting to read by themselves.

Adam's Starling
by Gillian Perdue
O'Brien Press €6.50

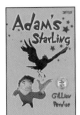

Adam is nine. He is finding life difficult but then he makes a special, secret friend in the form of a starling. Can Adam defend this new friend against the gang of bullies who have been making his life a misery? Perdue was a primary school teacher and clearly knows her stuff. A thoughtful book about bullying, with a light touch, which won the Eilis Dillon Award in 2002.

The Adventures of Captain Underpants (Reluctant Readers)
by Dav Pilkey
Scholastic €7.70

Dav Pilkey is an American teacher and he clearly understands how boys tick. By giving them funny and rather rude books to read, he has turned many a reluctant reader into a bookworm. Stuffed with fart and underpants jokes, they are not for the faint hearted. They're big, brash, silly, furiously paced and lots of fun. With zany black and white cartoon illustrations. Also good for older readers with short attention spans.

Horrid Henry Series (Reluctant Readers)
by Francesca Simon
Orion €7.70

Henry is always getting into trouble at home and in school, and for good reason as he is impossible. He likes nothing better than screaming and shouting, and loves antagonising other children, not to mention adults. A must for any child who's a bit of a horror, or who likes reading about one. Not for the easily offended. Great black and white illustrations by Tony Ross throughout. Read aloud if you dare. Great for reluctant readers, especially boys.

Ottoline and the Yellow Cat
by Chris Riddell Macmillan €13.85

Miss Ottoline Brown lives in a stylish apartment in Big City with a hairy creature called Mr Munroe. Together they look after the Brown family's rather eccentric collection and dabble in a spot of detective work on the side. In this book, they expose an ingenious 'dognapping' scam run by the furry feline crook, Yellow Cat. This beautiful looking book will appeal to any stylish young reader who likes their mysteries and adventure stories to be quirky and original. Exceptional illustrations.
Also by this author/illustrator: *Hugo Pepper; Fergus Crane*

Mr Gum and the Biscuit Billionaire (Reluctant Readers)
by Andy Stanton   Egmont €7.70

A cross between Roald Dahl and Monty Python, this book will have you crying with laughter and it's perfect for reluctant readers too. You'll meet a gingerbread man called Alan Taylor, an evil butcher, Jake the dog and an angry bathtub fairy and there are jokes heaped upon jokes. Sounds crazy? Oh, the plot is completely lunatic and the writing scarily mad, but somehow it all works! It'll brighten your day. Winner of the Guardian Children's Fiction Prize, 2007.
Also by this author: *You're a Bad Man, Mr Gum!*

The Owl Who Was Afraid of the Dark (Read Aloud)
by Jill Tomlinson
Egmont 6.15

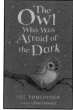

A gentle, atmospheric story about a barn owl, Plop, who is afraid of the dark. Everyone he meets has a good reason for liking the dark and gradually he learns that night-time isn't so bad after all. A sweet, reassuring story for younger readers which also makes a great read aloud. Especially good for children who are interested in the natural world. Over twenty years old now, this book is still a winner.
Also by this author: *The Hen Who Wouldn't Give Up*

Astrid, the Au Pair from Outer Space
by Emily Smith
Young Corgi €6.15

This is an entertaining and imaginative tale about Astrid, a very strange kind of au pair. When she admits she's an alien, her young charge, Harry, starts to worry that she's going to leave her new family. After all, he's getting quite fond of her, even if she is from outer space. A well observed, cleverly written story of family life, albeit odd family life, with tender, gentle humour and nicely rounded characters, even the alien ones.

The Hundred-Mile-an-Hour Dog
by Jeremy Strong
Puffin €6.15

This book won the Children's Book Award and is a funny, irreverent story featuring a mad dog called Streaker and his patient owner, Trevor. Trevor has until the end of his holidays to train Streaker or he'll lose his bet with the horrible and wonderfully named Charlie Smugg. Great black and white illustrations by the talented Nick Sharratt.
Also by this author: *Beware! Killer Tomatoes*

Lizzie Zipmouth
by Jacqueline Wilson
Young Corgi €6.15

Lizzie refuses to speak to her new stepbrothers, their dad, Sam, or even her own mum. She doesn't want to join a 'new' family and nothing can make her speak to them until she meets a new member of the family who is even more stubborn than she is. Wilson is known for her gritty, funny stories for older readers and this book for younger readers is no different. It deals with a real situation with humour and honesty.

The Cat Mummy ★
by Jacqueline Wilson
Young Corgi €7.70

This is one of my favourite Jacqueline Wilson books for younger readers. Verity's old tabby cat, Mabel, used to belong to her mother, who is now dead. When Verity finds Mabel dead in her wardrobe, she decides to mummify her so that she can keep the cat forever. I know it all sounds a bit morbid, but the animal's death is dealt with gently and with simple, searing honesty which children (and adults) respect. Through dealing with the death of her much loved cat, Verity also learns to deal with her mother's death. A graceful and thoughtfully written book. I love it.

OTHER AUTHORS TO LOOK OUT FOR:

ADVENTURE TALES:
Gillian Cross
Natalie Jane Prior
Penelope Lively

FUNNY STORIES:
Ian Whybrow
Shoo Rayner
Stephanie Dagg
Conor McHale
Humphrey Carpenter

FAMILY STORIES:
Berlie Doherty
Annie Dalton

ANIMAL STORIES:
Sam McBratney
Gordon Snell
Ursula Moray Williams

GIFT BOOKS AND CLASSICS FOR SLIGHTLY OLDER CHILDREN OF 5/6+

The Little Prince
by Antoine de Saint-Exupery
Egmont €15.40 H/Bk, €9.25 P/Bk

A French classic, *The Little Prince* has enthralled children and adults of all ages since it was first published in 1943. Illustrated by the author, who was a pilot, it's a charming examination of what it means to be human. For parents and children with a slightly philosophical nature.

Illustration © 1999 Helen Oxenbury. From *Alices's Adventures in Wonderland* by Lewis Carroll, illustrated by Helen Oxenbury. Reproduced by permission of Walker Books.

Alice's Adventures in Wonderland
by Lewis Carroll; illustrated by Helen Oxenbury
Walker Books €23.10

A new edition of this classic tale, with fresh, lively watercolour illustrations by Helen Oxenbury, bringing Alice alive to a whole new generation of children. Ideal for reading aloud, this attractive book is a must for any older child's bookshelves, including those named 'Alice'.
Also by this illustrator: *Alice Through the Looking Glass*

The Wind in the Willows
by Kenneth Grahame
illustrated by Inga Moore
Walker Books €23.10

The classic tale of Mole, Ratty, Badger and, of course, the exasperating Toad, is brought to glowing life by Inga Moore's stunning illustrations. This book has charmed generations of children (and adults) since 1908 and it is still as entertaining and as relevant as ever. A witty tale of friendship, it makes an enchanting read aloud for the slightly older child of five or six plus. Also available with illustrations by E H Shepard of Winnie the Pooh fame.

IRISH LEGENDS AND STORIES – PICTURE BOOKS AND GIFT BOOKS

The Sleeping Giant
by Marie Louise Fitzpatrick
Merlin €6.99

This delightful picture book won a Bisto Book of the Year Award in 1992. A gentle giant lies fast asleep off the coast of Dingle for hundreds of years until one day he wakes up with delightful consequences. A sweet and funny tale with bright, vibrant watercolour illustrations.

Tales from Old Ireland
by Malachy Doyle
illustrated by Niamh Sharkey
Barefoot Books €15.40

Seven traditional Irish tales are illustrated in a wonderfully quirky manner by Niamh Sharkey in this handsome book. From Fair, Brown and Trembling to The Children of Lir, Niamh's strong yet muted colours make the lyrically written stories come alive. A lovely collection to read aloud to an older child of five or six plus.

Irish Legends for Children
by Yvonne Carroll and Lucy Su
Gill and Macmillan €6.15

A useful introduction to Irish legends for younger children. All the old favourites are here, from the Children of Lir, to the Salmon of Knowledge, and of course, Oisín in Tír na nÓg. The illustrations are brightly coloured and child friendly.
Also by this author: *Great Irish Legends for Children*

Stories for Children ★
by Oscar Wilde, illustrated by P J Lynch   Hodder €15.40

Beautifully written, timeless and moving, Oscar Wilde's children's stories should be read to every Irish child. The stories include 'The Happy Prince' who gives up everything for his friend; and 'The Selfish Giant' who learns to love children and to share his fabulous walled garden. The illustrations by celebrated Irish illustrator P J Lynch are magical. Another great book to read to an older child.
Also by this illustrator: *When Jessie Came Across the Sea; The Christmas Miracle of Jonathan Twomey; Ignis; A Christmas Carol*

Illustration © P J Lynch. From *The Christmas Miracle of Jonathan Twomey*, illustrated by P J Lynch. Reproduced by permission of Walker Books.

By eight or nine most readers have mastered the mechanics of reading and are ready to move on to longer books with more complicated plots and longer chapters. Every child is different. There are books in this section to suit all tastes – funny books, sad books, historical books, thoughtful books, fast-paced action adventures.

The important thing is to keep them reading. Books on tape and cd are also great for this age. My son listens to a book on tape every night before he goes to sleep, after reading for a while. He enjoys it and it also builds up his vocabulary and word skills. He can also listen to books he finds too long and wordy to read for himself.

Sometimes children don't take to reading as much as we would like them to. These reluctant readers are often boys. They might enjoy comics and graphic novels, like Tin Tin and Asterix, or even history books and sports biographies. The Captain Underpants series by Dav Pilkey (reviewed on page 45) is also excellent for reluctant readers; as are Roddy Doyle's witty children's books, reviewed on page 39. **The novels that might interest the more reluctant reader are marked RR beside the title.** There are also some reviews of the Barrington Stoke books on page 73, especially written, designed and published for older children who find reading difficult.

Let your children see **you** reading. They need to see you engaging with books and enjoying your own reading. The recent success of 'crossover books' (children's books which are also read and enjoyed by adults) like THE BOY IN THE STRIPED PYJAMAS and THE CURIOUS INCIDENT OF THE DOG IN THE NIGHT-TIME has shown that adults enjoy reading children's books too. Some of the very best and most innovative writing today is between the covers of books for children and teenagers.

Woof!
by Allan Ahlberg
Puffin €7.70

Eric goes to sleep one night and wakes up as a dog. Throughout the day, he keeps changing from dog to boy and back again, causing all sorts of problems. With help from his best friend, Roy, he must discover the secret behind his strange situation. A very funny book which moves along at a nice, lively pace. Also good for reading aloud.

Also by this author: *The Giant Baby*

Chasing Vermeer
by Blue Balliett
Chicken House €9.25

Reviewed by Amanda, Dubray Books, Blackrock

A Vermeer painting is stolen. Two bright, quirky sixth graders come together to solve the crime that has the whole world baffled. Going beyond a simple mystery, this story explores the meaning of art and the nature of coincidence. A tale of action, adventure and suspense. Highly recommended.

The Palace of Laughter
by John Berkeley
Simon and Schuster €13.85

Miles Wednesday is an orphan who lives in a barrel. When he meets silver-winged acrobat, Little, they decide to follow the Circus Oscuro; he to find his stuffed bear, Tangerine, she to find Silverpot, an angel. Their quest leads them to the Palace of Laughter, a place where fun is strictly forbidden. This is a classic adventure yarn with lots of very inventive characters and a gripping plot, from a new Irish author. Shortlisted for the Bisto Award 2007.

The Indian in the Cupboard
by Lynne Reid Banks
HarperCollins €7.70

Omri is given an old plastic Indian and a small wooden cupboard for his birthday. When the Indian in placed in the cupboard, he comes to life and gets up to all sorts of mischief, and Omri has to try and keep him out of trouble. A delightfully funny, action packed story for boys and girls with a sense of adventure.

Are You There, God? It's Me, Margaret
by Judy Blume Macmillan €7.70

Reviewed by Lynn, Dubray Books, Grafton Street, Dublin

Growing up isn't easy and Margaret is just beginning to find this out for herself. She's just moved house which means starting from scratch in a new school and trying to make new friends. As if that isn't enough, she has to decide whether to become a Christian or a Jew and is worried about the fact that she hasn't got her period yet. But even when she's all alone, she can always talk to God. Funny and realistic.

The Famous Five
by Enid Blyton
Hodder €7.70

First published in the 1940s, this adventure series is now as popular as ever. Featuring four plucky children, Julian, Anne, George, Dick, and their dog, Timmy, these books are the perfect introduction to thrillers and adventure tales. Blyton wrote over six hundred titles in her life time but The Famous Five have remain her best loved books. (The Secret Seven titles are reviewed on page 36.)

Also by this author: St Clare's and Malory Towers school series

Billy Elliot (RR)
Melvin Burgess Chicken House €9.25

Books that have been adapted from film scripts can be poorly written, but this one is a notable exception. The story of a twelve-year-old boy from a coal mining family who discovers he has a talent for ballet, Burgess has managed to produce a cracking read. Billy's dad, Jackie, is not amused at his son's interest in dance but his ballet teacher, Mrs Wilkinson, is determined to help him. A gripping story about family conflict and following your dreams.

If you enjoyed this, you might also like *A Cuckoo in the Nest* by Michelle Magorian, about a boy who wants to be an actor.

Millions
by Frank Cottrell Boyce
Macmillan €9.25

This book draws you in right from the first page and doesn't let go. Damian Cunningham lives with his brother, Anthony, and his widowed dad. He's obsessed with saints and talks to them and about them all the time. One day, he finds a huge sack of stolen money and sets about trying to spend it with sometimes hilarious, sometimes worrying, results. Brilliantly funny and touching, this is a must read for older readers of age ten plus.
Also by this author:
Framed

age 8–12 years

Driftwood *
by Cathy Cassidy
Puffin €9.25

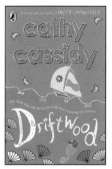

This book made me miss my train stop. I was so engrossed in it, my DART sailed past Pearse Street and I didn't even notice. I loved it. Hannah and Joey have been best friends forever. When Joey's new foster brother, Paul, starts to be bullied in school, the two friends try to help him, but sometimes people don't want to be rescued. A thoughtful and honest examination of bullying and not fitting in, with great characters you really warm to. The strong theme makes it suitable for a more mature reader of ten plus. Ideal for any Jacqueline Wilson fan.

Also by this author: *Scarlet; Indigo Blue; Dizzy; Sundae Girl; Lucky Star*

All About Cathy Cassidy

Cathy was born in 1962 in Coventry. She went to Art College in Liverpool, before landing the job as fiction editor on the legendary *Jackie* magazine (named after Jacqueline Wilson). Then she married her boyfriend, Liam, and went back to college and trained to be an art teacher. She now lives in Galloway, Scotland with her teenage children. As well as writing her novels, she is the agony aunt on Shout magazine and sometimes teaches art in the local primary schools, which she says keeps her sane. She is a vegetarian and loves old clothes, old toys, cars, and books.

All About Eoin Colfer

Eoin was born in Wexford in 1965 and has four brothers. He still lives in Wexford with his wife, Jackie, and their two sons, Finn and Sean. His first book, *Benny and Omar* (1998), was based in Tunisia, where he lived for several years. He was a primary school teacher before becoming a full time writer. In 2001, the first Artemis Fowl book was published, making him an instant international success. He says, 'I will keep writing until people stop reading or I run out of ideas. Hopefully neither of these will happen anytime soon.'

The Artemis Fowl Series ★ (RR)
by *Eoin Colfer* Puffin €10.75

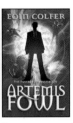

Described as 'Die Hard with Fairies', Colfer's hugely popular Artemis books are not to be missed. Action packed fantasy adventure stories, they're more James Bond than Lord of the Rings and are full of amazing spy gadgets, weapons and larger than life characters. In the first book, Artemis, the twelve-year-old criminal mastermind, is determined to rob the fairies of their gold but he's picked the wrong fairies to mess with. Enter Captain Holly Short of the LEPrecon Unit, the fairy police. The two match their wits with dangerous consequences. Brilliant, inventive, gripping. My favourite in the series of five books is *Artemis Fowl and the Lost Colony* but they are all dazzling reads.
Also by this author: *The Wish List; Benny and Omar; Benny and Babe*

Half Moon Adventures
by *Eoin Colfer* Puffin €10.75

Twelve-year-old private Detective Fletcher Moon is a wonderful creation, a flawed street-wise boy with a talent for wise cracks and a habit of getting into trouble. In this fast paced book he sets out to expose a well known Dublin mob family, the Sharkeys. But he soon realises that there's more to notorious child criminal, Red Sharkey, than meets the eye. A self proclaimed Raymond Chandler fan, Eoin's playful, hard boiled style is razor sharp and highly entertaining. This is an author at the height of his powers and having a whale of a time.

The Famine Trilogy ★
by Marita Conlon-McKenna
O'Brien Press €7.95

First published in 1990, *Under the Hawthorn Tree*, the first book in the Famine Trilogy, was on the Irish bestseller lists for over two years. It has been translated into dozens of languages and has also been filmed. Set in the 1840s during the Great Irish Famine, it brings history to technicolour life for its readers. Three brave children set out on a perilous journey to Castle Taggert and the safety of their aunts. A hugely involving tale of strength, courage and the will to survive. Don't miss it!

Also by this author: *Wildflower Girl; Fields of Home; The Blue Horse; A Girl Called Blue; No Goodbye; In Deep Dark Woods; Safe Harbour*

Marita Conlon-McKenna

Marita was born in Dublin in 1956 and now lives in Stillorgan with her husband, James McKenna, and their four children, Amanda, Laura, Fiona and James, and dog, Benji.

Marita, where did you get the idea for *Under the Hawthorn Tree*?

'Having heard a story about the skeletons of three young children from Famine times been unearthed in a field under a hawthorn tree, I couldn't get the story out of my head and every time I looked at my own four children I thought about those children of long ago.

I began to write this story at my kitchen table and the words came fast and furious. I literally wrote night and day as I was scared the story would run away from me. I knew that somehow I needed to make the connection between children in the present and the past. My family read and loved the story and urged me to send it to a publisher. I sent it to O'Brien Press and they decided to buy it. Within a very short time, they had sold rights for the *Under the Hawthorne Tree* all over the world.

Wonderful things keep happening with the book, like winning International Book Awards and being filmed by Young Filmmakers Ireland but, more importantly, children from every part of the globe have made it their own and are reading *Under the Hawthorn Tree* in their own language. It has been such a lucky book.'

Love that Dog ★
by *Sharon Creech*
Bloomsbury €7.70

Please, please, please buy this book for yourself; you'll get as much from this utterly wonderful novel as your child does. It never fails to warm my heart. It's written in the form of free verse (but don't let that put you off) and it tells the story of a boy who 'hates poetry' but gradually changes his mind. It's about all kinds of things but, most of all, it's about being human and the power of the imagination. Best of all, children love it too!

The Demon Headmaster
by *Gillian Cross*   Oxford €9.25

Dinah has just started a new school and from the very first day notices that things are a little strange. The pupils are all immaculately dressed and they even recite facts and figures while in the playground. Who or what are they afraid of, and what is the secret behind the terrifying headmaster? A delightfully sinister tale for any child who likes to be spooked.
Also by this author: *The Great Elephant Chase*

Alice Next Door
by *Judi Curtin*   O'Brien Press €7.95

Megan and Alice are best friends. They are in the same class in school, they live on the same road and they even like and dislike the same people. When Alice's parents separate and she has to move away, the two girls are distraught. But together they come up with a clever plan. A touching and funny story about the true nature of friendship. A good choice for any younger Jacqueline Wilson fan, there are several more books in the Alice series.
Also by this author: *Alice Again; Alice in the Middle; Don't Ask Alice*

Judi Curtin

MY 5 FAVOURITE CHILDREN'S BOOKS

1/ THE VOYAGE OF THE DAWN TREADER by CS Lewis. A magical book. What more can I say?

2/ HEIDI by Johanna Spyri. Wonderfully evocative. When I visited the Alps in summer a few years ago, I half-expected Heidi and her goats to skip past me.

3/ PEEPO by Janet and Allan Ahlberg. An early favourite for my own children, and one I never got tired of reading to them.

4/ WHAT KATY DID by Susan Coolidge. Katy was far from perfect – just the kind of character that little girls like to read about.

5/ FIRST TERM AT MALORY TOWERS by Enid Blyton. The book that made me want to go to boarding school.

Because of Winn-Dixie
by Kate Di Camillo
Walker €7.70

In small town Florida, lonely newcomer India finds friendship and solace when she adopts scraggy stray mutt Winn-Dixie. Through their escapades, this unlikely pair brighten lives and bring a community together. A poignant story of companionship and loyalty, Winn-Dixie will be capturing the hearts of children for generations to come.

Also by this author: *The Tale of Despereaux*

The Miraculous Journey of Edward Tulane
(One of Siobhán Parkinson's favourite authors)
by Kate Di Camillo
Walker Books €20.00

Reviewed by Edwina, Dubray Books, Stillorgan

Edward Tulane is a beautiful china rabbit whose heart is as cold as the china he is made from, until one day he is lost. Here begins Edward's and our extraordinary journey. This is a beautifully illustrated and wonderfully told story and is guaranteed to stay with you and your child long after the last page. A lovely gift for children of eight and upwards.

Matilda ★
by Roald Dahl Puffin €9.25

I adore Matilda. She's a genius but her parents pay her very little attention, worrying that she's far too fond of books for her own good. Only her teacher, Miss Honey, appreciates her quick wit and very special talents. Matilda uses her psychic powers to save the children in her school from the horrible head, Miss Trenchbull. Subversive, zany and very funny, this is wonderful stuff and great for reading aloud. Unmissable. Excellent black and white illustrations by Quentin Blake.

Also by this author: *Charlie and the Chocolate Factory; James and the Giant Peach*

Danny the Champion of the World
by Roald Dahl Puffin €9.25
Reviewed by Lynn, Dubray Books, Grafton Street, Dublin

As a child I loved the twisted humour of The Twits and The Witches but this book really won me over as a true Roald Dahl fan. 'Danny' is the story of a young boy, his father and the illegal practice of pheasant poaching. I was transfixed from the very first page. It kept my heart racing and my imagination flying throughout. It's an absolutely superb read and one that exposes parents as human too – an exciting revelation for all young readers!

The Spiderwick Chronicles
by Tony DiTerlizzi and Holly Black Simon and Schuster €10.75

Reviewed by Mary, Dubray Books, Galway

The Grace children, Mallory, Simon and Jared, move from their city apartment into a ramshackle family mansion after their parents' divorce. They discover a hidden attic room, a well-researched field guide on fairies and elves, and that they are not living alone on the family estate. Delightfully written, there is a strong sense of each character's personality and a real sense of adventure in everyday life. Fantasy with the innocence and acceptance of childhood.

The Neverending Story
by Michael Ende Puffin €12.30

Reviewed by Susan, Marketing and Promotions Manager, Dubray Books

This captivating story left a lasting impression on me as a child and remained for many years 'The Best Book I Ever Read'. The friendless and lonely Bastian hides away in his school attic with a stolen book and finds himself becoming part of a thrilling fantasy adventure through its pages. The world Fantastica is dying along with all its wonderful characters – the childlike Empress, the young warrior Atreyu, the Luck Dragon and the wonderful Falkor. All they need is one small boy to realise that the stories you read in books can be just as real as they are in your imagination. Cherish your copy and pass it on to your grandkids.

Flour Babies
by Anne Fine Puffin €9.25

A well written, touching and very funny tale of a class of boys who have to pretend to be parents for a school project. Each boy is given a sack of flour to look after as if it was a baby. Mayhem ensues and the boys learn that being a dad isn't as easy as it looks. A brilliant idea, well executed and a book that deserves to be read. Anne Fine also wrote the wonderful and thought provoking Madame Doubtfire (filmed as Mrs Doubtfire with Robin Williams). **Also by this author:** *Goggle Eyes; The Granny Project*

Harriet the Spy
by Louise Fitzhugh
HarperCollins €10.75

This is another of my favourite children's books of all time. The touching story of Harriet who has a secret spy notebook, it is brilliantly written and bursts with life. When her notebook is found by a girl in school, Harriet's friends and class mates are angry and upset at her very honest and sometimes cutting spy 'observations'. But slowly, with the help of her clever nanny she manages to redeem herself. Perfect for any child who has ever felt different.

The Thief Lord
by Cornelia Funke
Chicken House €10.75

Reviewed by Mary, Dubray Books, Galway

Set in Venice, Prosper and Bo have run away and are seeking shelter in a disused cinema. They are soon befriended by a gang of street children and their leader, Scipio, the Thief Lord. Pursued by a bungling detective, the children are hired by a mysterious Comte to steal a precious magical object that has the unique ability to spin or move time. A gripping read; fast-paced, loaded with suspense and adventure. Well-grounded in the real, this is a fantasy with a quirky twist. Cornelia Funke is a brilliant writer.

Also by this author: *Dragon Rider; Inkheart*

If you enjoyed this you might like *Stravaganza* by Mary Hoffman, also set in Venice.

The Asterix Adventures (RR)
by Rene Goscinny and Albert Uderzo
Orion €10.75

Asterix, the cunning and small warrior and his friend, Obelix, a man mountain, are the heroes of over twenty classic cartoon books about the last Gaulish tribe to remain undefeated by the Romans. Each book is a fantastic blend of adventure, battles, quests, magic potions and cringe-worthy and hilariously bad jokes. The brilliant illustrations are full of action, not to mention emotion and humour. Wonderful for any adventure or humour fan of eight plus.

If you like Asterix, you might also like *The Tin Tin Adventures* by Hergé.

I Am David
by Anne Holm   Mammoth €7.70

This is an extraordinary tale of hope, courage and adventure. David has spent all his young life in a concentration camp and doesn't know how to smile. When a guard helps him to escape, living on his wits he has to travel alone across Europe to find his family. A beautifully written story that inspires real emotion in its readers. Perfect for any child who has read and enjoyed *The Boy in the Striped Pyjamas* or who has an interest in history.

Double or Die (Young Bond)
by Charlie Higson   Puffin €10.75

Young James Bond finds himself investigating the mysterious disappearance of one of his teachers at Eton. A suspicious letter crammed with cryptic clues arrives and James must crack the code, then has just forty-eight hours to save the professor from the dark forces that threaten to destroy them both and maybe the whole world. An action packed adventure story, this well written book has a real sense of danger and peril. Perfect for Anthony Horowitz fans.
Also by this author: *Silverfin; Blood Fever*

Anthony Horowitz

10 THINGS YOU DIDN'T KNOW ABOUT
ANTHONY HOROWITZ

1. Anthony began writing because he wanted to be like Tintin.

2. He has travelled to all the places in the Tintin books (except the moon).

3. Snatchmore Hall (in THE SWITCH) is based on the house where Anthony lived as a child. He had a nanny, two cooks, two gardeners, a chauffeur – and he hated it.

4. He was sent to a revolting boarding school, Orley Farm, in north London. The headmaster and his wife featured by name in one of his TV episodes. He depicted them as mad Nazis!

5. He takes research for his books very seriously. He has walked across the Andes and visited the Forbidden City in Hong Kong. For POINT BLANC, he climbed – and operated – a 150m crane opposite the Houses of Parliament.

6. He got married in Hong Kong. He didn't understand the ceremony because it was in Chinese.

7. He spent a year working as a cowboy in Australia. This was for fun – not for a book.

8. His passion is scuba-diving. He has dived all over the world, including Sipadan in the South China Sea, where he saw hammerhead sharks.

9. He has a chocolate-coloured labrador called Lucky. Lucky by name, but not by nature – the dog has been run over three times!

10. He is a major film fan and goes to the cinema three or four times a week. His favourite film is THE THIRD MAN. He is also a big fan of Alfred Hitchcock's mysteries.

Stormbreaker ★ (RR)
by Anthony Horowitz
Walker €10.75

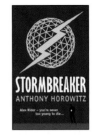

This is the first book in the hugely popular Alex Rider series about a fourteen-year-old spy. Already an orphan, when Alex's guardian is killed, he finds himself forcibly recruited into the MI6 as a spy. His first mission throws him into mortal danger and it takes all his courage to come out of it alive. A thrilling, action-packed story for all adventure fans. Alex is a charming and witty hero and these books make compelling reading. **Also by this author:** *Granny; The Falcon's Malteser; Ark Angel; Point Blanc; Snakehead; Scorpia; Skeleton Key; Eagle Strike; Night Rise; Evil Star*

Journey to the River Sea
by Eva Ibbotson
Macmillan €9.25

Maia, a feisty and adventurous orphan, is sent to stay with her relatives in the heart of the Amazon jungle. Her twin cousins turn out to be horribly spoilt and her aunt hates the jungle and all its creepy crawlies but, together with her wonderful governess, Miss Minton, Maia manages to find the kind of adventures that she's always dreamed about. Magical and beautifully written, this charming book makes a captivating read aloud choice.

Also by this author: *The Secret of Platform 13; The Morning Gift*

Redwall
by Brian Jacques
Red Fox €10.75

This classic fantasy adventure series set in the animal world was first published in 1986 and is still entertaining children to this day. Featuring Redwall Abbey and its brave mice and woodland creatures, it's a fun, fast paced read. Evil lurks in the form of Cluny the Scourge (a one-eyed rat). The Redwall inhabitants must band together to save the Abbey from destruction. Perfect for readers who like a good fight scene.

When Hitler Stole Pink Rabbit
by Judith Kerr
HarperCollins €9.25

Based on Kerr's own war time experiences, this is a thrilling, involving story of escape and danger. Anna and her family escape from the Nazis and go on the run, encountering evil and hardship along the way, but always keeping their sense of humour. Well written and gripping, an excellent choice for any history lover or for any reader who just likes a good adventure story which is a little bit different.

Howl's Moving Castle
by Diana Wynne Jones   HaperCollins €9.25

Reviewed by Aisling, Dubray Books, Grafton Street, Dublin

This author is a favourite of mine. Her stories are amazingly imaginative and *Howl's Moving Castle* in particular has all the ingredients of a classic Grimm's fairy tale with some added dimensions. This story is about a moving castle, three sisters, a witch, a demon and a magician. The magic, mystery and mayhem are all woven beautifully together to make a brilliant story. A wonderful book by a highly original author who is often overlooked. Perfect for any younger Potter fans.

Also by this author: *The Worlds of Chrestomanci*

Photograph – HarperCollins

Face to Watch: Derek Landy

Derek Landy lives in Lusk in North Co Dublin with his Alsatian, Ali. Before writing Skullduggery Pleasant, he wrote the screenplay for a zombie movie, *Boy Eats Girl*, and a slasher thriller, *Dead Bodies*, in which everybody dies.

As a black belt in Kenpo Karate, he has taught countless children how to defend themselves, in the hopes of building his own private munchkin army. He firmly believes that they await his call to strike against his enemies (he doesn't actually have any enemies but he's assuming they'll show up sooner or later). He says it really informs his fight scenes in the book. It also opened his eyes about teenagers. 'They're really smart. Much smarter than me!'

His written dialogue is heavily influenced by films of the forties, especially the movies of Howard Hawks, from *Bringing Up Baby* to *The Big Sleep* and there's a lot of the Cary Grant in his suave skeleton detective. *Skulduggery* popped into Derek's head in the summer of 2005 when he was in a hotel room in London, after a meeting with some film producers. By the end of December he'd finished the book. And now he's one of the hottest new children's authors around. Watch this space.

Skulduggery Pleasant ★ (RR)
by Derek Landy
HarperCollins €10.75

Set in modern day Dublin, this is a brilliant fantasy adventure novel featuring Stephanie, a thirteen-year-old who is full of attitude, and her friend, the skeleton detective, Skulduggery. Together they must uncover the mystery of her uncle's death, encountering flocks of wonderfully larger than life evil characters along the way. *Skulduggery Pleasant* is taut, full of zippy dialogue and fantastically inventive and will thrill any Harry Potter or Artemis Fowl lover.

Attica
by Gary Kilworth
Atom €9.25

When Chloe, Jordy and Alex climb into the attic of their new home, looking for a pocket watch belonging to a previous tenant, they find another world. A world full of strange inhabitants, where nothing is quite as it seems; but how are they going to find the attic trapdoor and get back home? The wonderful characterisation and the strong writing really set this book apart. Recommended by writer Neil Gaiman, this is a brilliant fantasy adventure story.

The Thieves of Ostia:
Book 1 of The Roman Mysteries
by Caroline Lawrence
Orion €10.75

Set in 79AD this is a thrilling and fascinating tale about Flavia Gemina, a young Roman girl who loves solving mysteries. When her father's precious signet ring is stolen, she's determined to find the thief and she finds some new friends along the way: a Jewish/Christian boy called Jonathan, an African slave called Nubia, and a wild boy called Lupus who lives on the streets and has no tongue. An exciting and realistic look at life during the Roman Empire.
Also in this series: The Secrets of Vesuvius; The Pirates of Pompeii

The Young Rebels
by Morgan Llywelyn
O'Brien Press €7.95

Reviewed by Aisling, Dubray Books, Grafton Street, Dublin

This is an excellent read, set in the run up to and during the 1916 Easter Rising in Dublin. John Joe's life changes dramatically when he is sent to St Enda's boarding school by his father. Here he encounters Pádraig Pearse, Pearse's family and many others involved in preparing for the rebellion. Llwellyn gives us an amazing and insightful look into these characters and their actions, making you wish that you too could have spent time in their company. A stirring, mournful yet exciting read.

The Narnia Chronicles
by C S Lewis HarperCollins €9.25

These wonderful fantasy adventure tales have stood the test of time. The Lion, the Witch and the Wardrobe – the second book in the seven book series – is the best known but they are all great reads. When Peter, Susan, Edmund and Lucy take their first steps into the world behind the fur coats in the magic wardrobe, little do they realise what adventures are about to unfold. An unforgettable book which makes a perfect read aloud for a younger child.

Peter Pan in Scarlet
by Geraldine McCaughrean Oxford University Press €10.75

This sequel to J M Barrie's classic tale was written for modern readers by one of England's most respected children's writers. Wendy and the Lost Boys are now adults with families of their own but they are all having deeply disturbing dreams about Neverland and the terrible things that are happening there. So they decide to return and see if they can help Peter put things to right. There's plenty of action and adventure along the way. Well written and cleverly plotted.

Also by this author: *Stop the Train*

Kensuke's Kingdom
by Michael Morpurgo Egmont €7.70

Michael is washed overboard from his parents' yacht in the middle of the Pacific and finds himself stranded on a desert island with his dog, Stella. He thinks he is all alone and doomed, but soon realises there is someone watching over him, Kensuke. An exciting story about survival against the odds, friendship and trust. A good old fashioned adventure yarn in the tradition of Robinson Crusoe and Treasure Island with a modern twist that makes an excellent read aloud choice.

Also by this author: *The Wreck of the Zanzibar; The Amazing Story of Adolphus Tips*

I Believe in Unicorns
by Michael Morpurgo Walker Books €7.70
Reviewed by Edwina, Dubray Books, Stillorgan

Thomas does not like to read; in fact he hates to read. One day he finds himself banished to the library and he becomes enthralled by the magical stories of the 'Unicorn Lady'. Soon he finds himself visiting as often as possible until a war tears apart all that he knows and loves. This is a book about loss and survival under the hardest of circumstances, an enchanting story for any child of eight plus.

The Borrowers ★
by Mary Norton
Puffin €10.75

Reviewed by Mary, Dubray Books, Galway

The Borrowers are tiny people who live under the floorboards, behind mantelpieces and inside grandfather clocks. 'Borrowing' from the human world, however, is filled with dangers. They may be seen by the giant humans, or worse, hunted by cats. But what happens when young Arriety befriends a human boy? A modern classic, this is an excellent fantasy with a great sense of adventure and an understanding of what it means to be small in a very big world.

Second Fiddle
by Siobhán Parkinson
Puffin €7.70

Mags is still getting over her dad's death when she meets Gilliant, a talented violinist who needs money to attend an audition in England. After a rather shaky start the girls become friends. This book deals with some big issues – from divorce to bereavement – but they are deftly and realistically handled. This funny, well written book was shortlisted for the Bisto Award. Ideal for Jacqueline Wilson or Cathy Cassidy fans.
Also by this author:
Four Kids, Three Cats, Two Cows; Kate

Bridge to Terabithia ✶
by Katherine Patterson
Puffin €10.75

Reviewed by Amanda, Dubray Books, Blackrock

Two children become close friends and create a secret kingdom dubbed Terabithia. Yet their kingdom and friendship are short-lived when a tragedy strikes at the end of the story. A story that explores joy and sorrow as it deals with themes of friendship and loss. An essential masterpiece for any young reader's collection. Winner of the Newbery Medal in the US.

Tom's Midnight Garden ✶
by Philippa Pearse
Puffin €7.70

In my humble opinion this is one of the best children's books ever written. Tom's brother has the measles so Tom is sent to stay with his uncle and aunt during the summer holidays. One night, the grandfather clock in the hall strikes thirteen and a strange and mysterious garden appears. A rich and inventive story about the nature of time, growing old, friendship and ghosts. Beautifully written and utterly compelling, this book makes a delightful read aloud. Magical, moving, timeless; don't miss it!

Wolf Brother
by Michelle Paver   Orion €10.75

Reviewed by Mary, Dubray Books, Galway

Torak is an outcast from the Clans, alone in the world apart from a wolf cub whose life he spared. The wolf acts as companion and animal/spirit guide as Torak travels to the mythical Mountain of the World Spirit in order to save the people, and himself, from a giant demon in the form of a man-eating bear. Exceptionally intelligent, Paver provides us with a believable view of life 6,000 years ago. An eloquent coming-of-age epic, with struggle and triumph over impossible circumstances. The first in a six part series.
Also by this author: *Spirit Walker; Soul Eater*

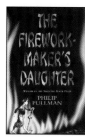

The Firework-Maker's Daughter
by Philip Pullman
Corgi €7.70

Lila lives 'a thousand miles away, in a country east of the jungle and south of the mountains'. She wants to be a firework-maker, like her father, but he thinks it's no job for a young girl. So she goes on an exciting adventure to discover the secrets of making a firework. A vital, lively story about courage and chasing your dreams which explodes onto the page, this book also makes a great read aloud.
Also by this author: *Clockwork*

Bill and Fred?
by John Quinn
O'Brien Press €7.95

This is a charming story about two eccentric sisters, 'Bill' and 'Fred', and their quirky outlook on life. Their old house is in terrible disrepair and needs a lot of work done to it so Fred decides to enter a local snooker competition and win the prize money, with hilarious consequences. Their young neighbour, Katie, is fascinated by the sisters and the three become firm friends. A delightfully warm and gentle story, beautifully written, about community, friendship and being different (at any age).

Swallows and Amazons
by Arthur Ransome
Red Fox €12.30

Set in the Lake District, this is a classic tale of childhood adventure. Four children, Titty, John, Roger and Susan spend the summer messing about in boats and camping on the local Wild Cat Island. When they are threatened by local 'pirates' they must pull together and prove their worth. A good humoured, charmingly old fashioned adventure story which makes a great read aloud.

Mortal Engines
by Philip Reeve
Scholastic €9.25

This is an exciting science-fiction adventure story set in London in the future. The city is now a Traction City, a seven-tiered metropolis mounted on huge treads, rolling over the wastelands of Europe, looking for smaller cities to eat up. Then along comes fifteen-year-old Tom Natsworthy, who along with a disfigured girl called Hester Shaw, has to catch up with the city as it rolls along. Gripping, inventive and full of surprises.
Also by this author: *Larklight; Predator's Gold*

The Riverside Series (RR)
by Peter Regan Children's Press

The Riverside books have delighted children for many years. In *Riverside: The Spy*, seventeen-year-old Jimmy is now managing the boys' football team and faces all the dilemmas that big league managers have, like who to play and how to win. But a spy in the team is giving away their secret strategies to a rival team. Good fun for soccer fans.

Percy Jackson and the Lightning Thief
by Rick Riordan Penguin €9.25

Reviewed by Amanda, Dubray Books, Blackrock

Percy has managed to get expelled from every school he has attended but things are looking up at his new school. Then disaster strikes. He learns he is the son of a mortal woman and one of the gods of Ancient Greek Mythology. He spends the rest of the story facing, fighting and fleeing various monsters including Medusa. An amazing book, full of intrigue and suspense.

Also by this author: *Percy Jackson and the Sea of Monsters*

Harry Potter ★
by J K Rowling
Bloomsbury €9.25 (in paperback)

What can I say about Harry Potter that hasn't already been said? JK Rowling deserves our eternal gratitude for helping a whole generation of children to become readers for life. Books and reading have never been so popular and the huge success of her boy wizard series has a lot to do with this. My favourite is book two, Harry Potter and the Chamber of Secrets, the giant spider, the flying car, the strange whispering in the walls, the wonderful characters you grow to love and care about, the edge of the seat plotting – outstanding, thrilling, addictive, unnerving, magical. Discover your own favourite.

   If you like Harry Potter you might also like:
Skulduggery Pleasant by Derek Landy
Artemis Fowl by Eoin Colfer
The Percy Jackson Tales by Rick Riordan
The Alchemyst by Michael Scott

How to Eat Fried Worms (RR)
by Thomas Rockwell Orchard €7.70

This is a wonderful book for boys who like a good laugh. It's also ideal for more reluctant readers as it's fast and easy to read. The story of a gang of boys who dare their friend, Billy, to eat more and more worms in lots of different 'recipes', this is witty, irreverent, and plain old-fashioned fun. First published in 1973, I haven't met a boy yet who doesn't find it hilarious. And if it keeps them reading, excellent.
   If you like this, you might also like *The Killer Underpants* by Michael Lawrence (RR)

Holes (RR)
by Louis Sacher Bloomsbury €10.75

Reviewed by Olivia, Dubray Books, Kilkenny

When unlucky Stanley Yelnats is sent to a prison camp for a crime he didn't commit, he encounters an unlikely group of friends. Follow his adventures through Camp Green Lake as he tries to make the best of his bad situation. A highly enjoyable read from an accomplished author, with lots of delightful twists and turns. Easy to read, it is a funny, fast moving book, which makes a great choice for more reluctant readers.

Ballet Shoes
by Noel Streatfeild Puffin €9.25

Reviewed by Mary, Dubray Books, Galway

Pauline, Petrova and budding ballerina Posey live a sheltered life caring for Great-Uncle Matthew's enormous fossil collection while he is away on expeditions. One day, both their uncle and the money he sends to provide for them disappear. The girls become students at the Children's Academy for Dance and Stage Training. Here, they learn to earn their own way and chart their own course in life through stage productions. A beautiful, classic book about independence, responsibility and growing up; and dancing. **Also by this author:** *Dancing Shoes; Circus Shoes*

The Silver Sword
by Ian Serraillier Puffin €7.70

Reviewed by Olivia, Dubray Books, Kilkenny

It's the Second World War and Poland is a scene of destruction and desolation. When the Balicki family are separated, the three children must fend for themselves until they are reunited with their parents once more. This is an all too familiar tale, wonderfully told by the author. Based on real events that Serraillier witnessed growing up, this book is both thrilling and heart warming as it shows a success story amid the carnage. A modern classic.

A Series of Unfortunate Events ⭐ (RR)
by Lemony Snicket
Egmont €10.75

There are thirteen depressing and gloomy books in this highly original series. The Baudelaire children are orphaned when their parents are killed in a terrible fire. Klaus, Violet and baby Sunny must now go and live with the nasty and sinister Count Olaf. They manage to survive despite all the cold porridge, itchy clothes and dastardly plans to knock them off. Gloriously dark and different, children of a certain disposition adore these strange yet hilarious books.

Vampirates: Demons of the Deep
by Justin Somper
Simon and Schuster €9.25

A swashbuckling pirate tale for all adventure lovers. Conor and Grace are orphan twins who set sail in their dad's sailing boat to avoid being adopted by the town's busy-bodies. Their boat capsizes and each is picked up by a different ship – Conor wakes up to find himself on a pirate ship, Grace is on a ship with vampirates. Can they find each other before Grace is eaten? Full of larger than life characters and great fun.

The Edge Chronicles: Beyond the DeepWoods (RR)
by Paul Stewart and Chris Riddell
Corgi €9.25

The first book in this popular fantasy series tells the story of Twig, abandoned at birth and brought up by wood trolls, who goes on a quest to find out who he really is. It's full of amazing creatures, from flesh-eating trees to goblins and trolls, and the story is full of action and humour. The wonderful line drawings by Chris Riddell are extremely detailed and really add to the atmosphere of this book. Ideal for readers who need a little encouragement.

Charlotte's Web ⋆
by E B White
Puffin €9.25

Reviewed by Vivienne, Dubray Books, Rathmines

Enjoyed for over fifty years, this classic story tells how Wilbur the pig's life is saved by a young girl called Fern and an exceptionally clever spider called Charlotte. The conversations among the animals who live together in the barn are hilarious, especially those between naive Wilbur and sarcastic Charlotte, which had me laughing out loud. With a poignant but hopeful ending, this is a heart-warming story about the importance of loyal friendship.

Also by this author: *Stuart Little*

The Guns of Easter
by Gerard Whelan   O'Brien Press €7.95

This exciting book is set during the 1916 Easter Rising and tells of one family's courage and will to survive. Young Jimmy Conroy looks for food for his family, seeing death and violence all around. This book is written in strong and direct language and brings history alive. Winner of the Eilis Dillon Award for a First Novel.

Also by this author: *Dream Invader; Out of Nowhere (age 11+); War Children*

Jacqueline Wilson

Jacqueline Wilson has sold over twenty million books and is one of the most popular authors in the world. I recently got the chance to ask her some burning questions.

Jacqueline, you recently visited Ireland. Will you ever set one of your books here?
'I'd love to set a book in Ireland some time, but I think I'd have to live there for at least a year to make it sound as if I knew what I was talking about!'

You are known for your dedication to your fans. What's the longest signing session you've ever done?
'I think my longest signing session was at Bournemouth, where I signed for eight hours, up until midnight. The children were nearly falling asleep – and so was I. My bladder was about to bust too. Nowadays my events are mostly ticketed as sessions that long are too much of a strain for all of us.'

How long were the queues in Dublin?
'The queues were cleverly organised and regulated with up to 500 tickets given out, so they were between three and five hours long.'

How did you cope with the Irish names?
'Yes, Irish names are beautiful, but a nightmare when you try to spell them. I can manage Niamh and Aoife but then I start to flounder. Luckily, everyone writes their names on post-it notes stuck to the title page, so I can copy them down accurately.'

Which Irish authors do you enjoy reading?
'I used to like Patricia Lynch's books when I was a little girl. When I grew up Edna O'Brien's books meant a lot to me. I've just finished reading *Amongst Women* by John McGahern, which I greatly admired, though I thought the main character a total monster.'

Wilson's direct, clear writing draws you in and her clever, unflinching plots keep you glued to the pages. I'm an enormous fan. But do be careful, some of Wilson's books deal with pretty strong stuff, from mothers having nervous breakdowns (*The Illustrated Mum*), to abandoned babies (*The Dustbin Baby*), and bullying (*Bad Girls*).

The Girls in Love series is more suitable for teenagers (reviewed on page 84). If in any doubt, read the book before passing it on to your child. Like me, you might even get addicted to Jacqueline's books yourself.

The Story of Tracy Beaker
by Jacqueline Wilson
Corgi €9.25

This is one of my favourite of Jacqueline Wilson's titles, along with *The Suitcase Kid* and *The Cat Mummy*. Tracy lives in a children's home and she has a vivid imagination. This book is written as Tracy's diary and is a funny and touching account of her daily life. She's always waiting for her mum to come and collect her but, according to Tracy, she's too busy being a star in Hollywood. A touching and searingly honest book, bursting with energy and featuring one of Wilson's most engaging heroines. **Also by this author:** *Jacky Daydream; Vicky Angel; Best Friends.*

If you like Jacqueline Wilson, you might also like Cathy Cassidy.

OTHER AUTHORS AND BOOKS WE LOVE:

THRILLER / MYSTERY /
ADVENTURE:
Gordon Snell
Michael Hoeye
Anna Dale
Robert Swindells
Charles Ogden and Rick Carton
Hardy Boys Series
Nancy Drew Series

FAMILY / REAL LIFE:
Alice Hoffman
Jean Ure
Phyllis Reynolds Naylor

FANTASY / OTHER WORLDS:
Lloyd Alexander
Stuart Hill
Frances Hardinge
Cliff McNish
Nancy Farmer
Patricia Murphy
Jenny Nimmo
Angie Sage
Ian Ogilvy
Jan Mark
Sally Prue
Julia Goulding

HUMOUR:
Sam Llewellyn
Terry Deary
Georgia Byng
Jamie Rix
Deirdre Madden

ANIMAL TALES:
Lucy Daniels
Vivian French
S.F. Said
Lauren Brooke (horses)
Don Conroy

HISTORICAL:
Grace Cavendish
Veronica Bennett
Sally Gardner
Carlo Gebler
Theresa Tomlinson
Rosemary Sutcliff
Marilyn Taylor

WORLD ISSUES / OTHER CULTURES:
Karen Hesse
Kevin Kiely
Elizabeth Lutzeier

CLASSICS WE LOVE:

Puffin Classics feature a great range of wonderful stories from Little Women to The Jungle Book, all in paperback format. There are also other classics ranges, such as Oxford University Press who produce very handsome hardbacks.

Brilliant for reading aloud, these books have stood the test of time. Here are some of our favourites:

Little Women
by Louisa May Alcott

The Secret Garden
by Frances Hodgson Burnett

Just William
by Richmal Crompton

Stig of the Dump
by Clive King

The Jungle Book
by Rudyard Kipling

Dr Dolittle
by Hugh Lofting

The Call of the Wild
by Jack London

Anne of Green Gables
by L M Montgomery

The Railway Children
by E Nesbit

Black Beauty
by Anne Sewell

Treasure Island
by Robert Louis Stevenson

Pollyanna
by Eleanor H. Porter

What Katy Did
by Susan Coolidge

Tom Sawyer *and* **Huckleberry Finn**
by Mark Twain

Daddy Long Legs
by Jean Webster

101 Dalmations
by Dodie Smith

Little House in the Big Woods
by Laura Ingalls Wilder

The Little White Horse
(J K Rowling's favourite book as a child)
by Elizabeth Gouge

Peter Pan
by J M Barrie

Mary Poppins
by P L Travers

IRISH CLASSICS

The Island of Horses
by Eilis Dillon

The Turf Cutter's Donkey
by Patricia Lynch

The Flight of the Doves
by Walter Macken

The Fox Series
by Tom McCaughren

There is a wealth of brilliant books for older readers of eleven plus. At this age, readers tend to select their own books but they still need guidance and encouragement. Every child and teenager is different.

There are some books in this section that deal with strong themes and if you are concerned about the content it is always a good idea to ask advice from one of the Dubray Books children's booksellers or read the book before your child, or at the same time. I have found discussing books with my thirteen-year-old son a real pleasure and a great way to communicate.

This is an important stage in a young reader's life. They will never again have as much time to lose themselves in books. And they will never forget the books they read at this age. So finding them interesting, good, meaty and engaging books is quite a responsibility.

If your teen is not reading as much as you'd like them to, don't worry. Keep them in the reading habit – let them read whatever they like – comics, graphic novels, sports biographies, magazines. Sometimes teens get overwhelmed by the amount of reading they have to do in secondary school, and want or need a rest from books. Hopefully, they will come back to reading for pleasure in their own good time. After all, some adults only read on their holidays, or when they have free time.

I'd like to thank children's book expert **Robert Dunbar** for reviewing some of his favourite books for this section.

RELUCTANT READERS OF 11+ AND READERS WITH HIGH INTEREST AND LOW ABILITY:

BARRINGTON STOKE SERIES

The Barrington Stoke books are published especially for reluctant readers and readers who find the mechanics of reading difficult. They combine strong, interesting stories with easy to handle text and are especially good for boys. There is something to catch every reader's interest, and do ask our children's buyers for advice as they will happily order titles that are not in stock.

Some of our favourites are:

Hard Luck
by Mary Arrigan
€ 7.70
A moving story about a homeless boy, by an award winning Irish author. Interest Age 12+ Reading Age 8+

Donny Delgado: Private Detective
by Kevin Brooks
€ 7.70
A white-knuckle detective story from another award winning author. Interest Age 13+ Reading Age 8+

I See You Baby
by Kevin Brooks and Catherine Ford
€ 7.70
A gripping and intense thriller cum relationship novel from two huge talents of the teenage fiction scene. Interest Age 13+ Reading Age 8+

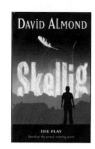

Skellig
by David Almond Hodder €12.30

Winner of the Guardian Award and the Carnegie Medal, this is a highly original and beautifully written story. Michael discovers a strange winged man in an old garage, a down and out creature who loves Chinese food. Can the man really be an angel and can he help save Michael's critically ill baby sister? With the help of his friend, Mina, Michael is determined to find out. An extraordinary, unpredictable, life affirming book.

Also by this author: *Kit's Wilderness*

Tuck Everlasting
by Natalie Babbitt
Bloomsbury €9.25

The Tuck family has a secret: they will all live forever thanks to the immortality spring they have sipped from. This does not make life any easier for them; in fact it makes it a lot harder and when young Winnie stumbles upon the secret, they are determined to prevent her from suffering the same fate. This is a beautifully written and highly original book which examines ageing, the value of life and the need to break away from family ties.

Abarat
by Clive Barker Voyager €10.75

This brilliant fantasy novel was recommended to me by Derek Landy, author of Skulduggery Pleasant. Candy Quackenbush lives in Chickentown, USA, the most boring town in the world. But fate is leading her to Abarat, a great archipelago of twenty five islands. There, helped by a cast of bizarre allies, she must fight the evil that is overtaking the islands. A dizzying and hugely imaginative ride that leaves most fantasy novels in the dust.

If you like Abarat, you might also like *Coraline* by Neil Gaiman.

Noughts and Crosses
by Malorie Blackman
Corgi €13.85

Crosses are black and Noughts are white. Crosses are rich and educated and Noughts have nothing. There is no equality in anything: politics, education, freedom and even love. In this strongly written and highly readable book, Blackman plays with the ideas of traditional racial stereotypes. Callum is a Nought and Sephy a Cross but they are in love and how can it be so wrong? A stirring love story combined with an interesting look at social justice.

Also by this author: *Knife Edge; Checkmate; The Stuff of Nightmares*

The Boy in the Striped Pyjamas ★
by John Boyne
Red Fox €10.75

Reviewed by Vivienne, Dubray Books, Rathmines

Nine-year-old German boy Bruno is not at all happy to learn that his father has been promoted and all the family are moving to the countryside. He soon finds himself with no one to play with but is curious about the many people he can see behind a fence in the distance. One day he sets off to explore and befriends a boy called Shmuel. This is a moving powerful story, simply and subtly told. An award winning must read.

If you liked this, you might also like *Once* by Morris Gleitzman or *Maus*, a graphic novel by Art Spigelman (reviewed on page 93).

All About John Boyne

10 THINGS YOU MIGHT NOT KNOW ABOUT JOHN BOYNE

1. I've broken 3 of my 4 limbs at different times.
2. I can say the alphabet backwards in less than 5 seconds.
3. I keep a list of every book I read and every movie I see.
4. I wrote the 1st draft of Striped Pyjamas in two and a half days, without sleep.
5. I've been up in a hot air balloon and one day I want to jump out of a plane. (With a parachute, of course)
6. My favourite book is DAVID COPPERFIELD by Charles Dickens.
7. I play guitar and piano. Badly.
8. When I was 12, I read the Narnia books from start to finish in two weeks while in hospital.
9. I can't whistle.
10. I make a mean spaghetti bolognese.

Starseeker (A Robert Dunbar Choice)
by Tim Bowler Oxford University Press €9.25
Reviewed by Robert Dunbar

Luke, a promising young musician, finds that his world is shattered by the death of his father. Falling in with bad company, he is forced into breaking into an old woman's house: this is the start of a series of experiences which are to have many revealing consequences for himself and his future.

Also by this author: *Midget; Storm Catchers; Apocalypse; Frozen Fire*

Faerie Wars
by Herbie Brennan
Bloomsbury €10.75

'Henry got up early on that day that changed his life'. So begins this dramatic fantasy adventure tale. After hearing that his dad is leaving the family home, fourteen-year-old Henry goes to find Mr Fogarty, the grumpy old man he works for, only to find a fairy in the shed. The fairy, Pygrus, needs his help. Soon Henry gets caught up in a dark and sinister plot to destroy the fairy world. Fast paced, entertaining and highly readable.

The Princess Diaries Series
by Meg Cabot
Macmillan €9.25

Meg Cabot is much loved by her legions of teenager readers, and for good reason. She has a lively, warm writing voice and her plots zip along in a good natured, skippy kind of way. In case you think these books are all sweetness and light, they aren't. Mia's life isn't easy, she's five foot nine and boys baffle her. Any teenager would sympathise with Mia and her very real problems. Good thoughtful fun.

If you like this series, you might also like *The Sisterhood of the Travelling Pants* by Anne Brashares

The Chocolate War
(A Robert Dunbar Choice)
by Robert Cormier
HarperCollins €10.75

Reviewed by Robert Dunbar

First published just over thirty years ago, this is now an accepted classic of teenage fiction. It deals with the bullying, exploitation and corruption rampant in an American high school and the efforts of one boy to defeat the system.

Walk Two Moons
by Sharon Creech
Macmillan €9.25

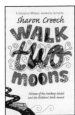

'Don't judge a man until you've walked two moons in his moccasins'. Another book I adore. Part teenage 'On the Road', part relationship novel, part examination of the nature of separation and grief, it is a stunning and compelling read. Salamanca Hiddle (Sal) goes on a road trip with her grandparents, retracing her mother's last journey. Along the way she learns the truth about her mother's life and death. Winner of the Newbery Medal in the US.
Also by this author: *The Wanderer; Ruby Holler*

The Black Tattoo
by Sam Enthoven
Doubleday €9.25

Jack and his best friend, Charlie, find themselves in a mysterious room over a theatre with some very strange characters. Charlie takes 'The Test' which leaves him with a Black Tattoo and a very bad temper. The boys and their new friend, martial arts expert, Esme, have to save the world from an evil monster, the Scourge. An epic tale of good and evil, influenced by comic books, martial arts and computer games, this is an action packed book no self-respecting teenage boy will want to miss. My thirteen-year-old son loved it.

The Louise Trilogy
by Aubrey Flegg
O'Brien Press €7.25 and €9.95

Wings Over Delft, the first book in this trilogy won the Bisto Book of the Year Award in 2004 and deservedly so. Set in seventeenth century Holland, it tells the story of Louise Eeden, the daughter of a local master potter. She's engaged to a childhood friend from a wealthy family but, when she reluctantly agrees to sit for a portrait, she meets Pieter, the painter's apprentice and begins to question her life. A beautifully written historical novel.

The Breadwinner
by Deborah Ellis
Oxford University Press €9.25

Parvana's father is arrested and four days later all the family's food has run out. Parvana must leave the house alone even though Taliban rule forbids it. She dresses up as a boy and has to dodge deadly landmines in her attempt to save her family from starvation. This topical book about a brave Afghan teenager brings home the real, human stories behind the headlines. A real eye opener.
Also by this author: *Parvana's Journey*

Coraline *
by Neil Gaiman   Bloomsbury €9.25

I read this wonderful, haunting book in one sitting. Coraline lives in part of a big old house with her parents and some eccentric neighbours. One day, she opens a door and goes into a parallel universe where everything seems (on the surface) to be much more interesting. But then strange things begin to happen, her family's life is threatened and Coraline must use all her wits to fight back. A fantastically creepy and highly original tale.

The Defender
(A Robert Dunbar Choice)
by Alan Gibbons
Orion €10.75

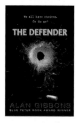

Reviewed by Robert Dunbar

An 'Ulster troubles' novel with a difference. Set mainly in the North of England, this is a story that demonstrates the long-term effects of a certain kind of Ulster upbringing and experience. Kenny Kincaid may have thought that in fleeing from Belfast he will be able to draw a line under his past, but when it dramatically catches up with him (and his son, Ian), he finds himself once more entangled in the repercussions of his earlier political involvements.

The Curious Incident of the Dog in the Night-Time *
by Mark Haddon
Red Fox €10.75

Reviewed by Vivienne, Dubray Books, Rathmines

I loved this book from the moment I picked it up and saw that the narrator describes, literally, what goes on in his mind. Christopher is 15 and has Asperger's syndrome, a type of autism. When his neighbour's dog is murdered, he takes on the role of detective. In attempting to solve the mystery, Christopher happens to make many discoveries about his family. This original novel gives an excellent insight into the thought processes of the character. A brilliant story.

Follow Me Down
by Julie Hearn
Oxford University Press €7.70

I couldn't put this extraordinary book down. This is a story that weaves together the past and the present in a clever and highly original way. Tom's mother has cancer, his gran has a nasty streak and, to add to all of this, he's started to hear voices. The voices lead him down to the cellar and back in time, to a world of freaks and a very special Changling Child. You'll never forget this chilling, uplifting and thought provoking book.
Also by this author: *Ivy; Hazel; The Merrybegot*

The Outsiders
by S E Hinton
Puffin €10.75

Hinton wrote this book when she was seventeen. Set in America in the 1960s, it's the story of Greasers and Socs (Socials) and their gang warfare. The Socs have it all and they make fun of Ponyboy Curtis and his friends, the Greasers, who come from the wrong side of town. Soon they have a 'rumble' and when Ponyboy's friend, Johnny, kills a Soc, he begins to question everything he's ever taken for granted. A gritty tale of revenge and regret. A teen classic.

The Journals Series
by various authors
O'Brien Press €7.95

An Irish series for teenagers featuring some strong women writers like Roisin Meaney and Judy May, these books are issues based and ideal for older Jacqueline Wilson fans. Don't Even Think About It by Roisin Meaney is the diary of Liz Jackson, a twelve-year-old latchkey kid, who loves Eminem and pizza but also hates the girl next door. A charming, fast paced story for younger teens with an attractive, fashionable cover.

Saffy's Angel
by Hilary McKay Hodder €9.25
Reviewed by Aoife, Dubray Books, Dun Laoghaire

This is the first novel in the Casson family series and is a great introduction to this delightfully quirky family. All the Casson children are named after colours on an artist's colour chart. However, one day, Saffy, short for Saffron, realises that her name isn't on the chart and subsequently discovers that she is adopted. When her grandfather dies, Saffy is prompted to embark on a quest to find something of her true origins. A laugh out loud story with many memorable characters.
Also by this author: *The Exiles in Love; Indigo's Star; Forever Rose*

The White Darkness (One of Kate Thompson's Favourite Books)
by Geraldine McCaughrean Oxford University Press €12.30

First love, obsession and loneliness with an Antarctic setting. Sym's dad is dead and she lives in a world of her own. Her Uncle Victor arranges a trip to the South Pole and McCaughrean describes the frozen landscape so wonderfully you shiver with every line. When things start to go wrong, Sym has to draw on all her inner strength and on the strange and glamorous Titus Oates. A rip-roaring, dazzlingly original adventure yarn with a delightfully chilly edge.
Also by this author: *The Kite Rider*

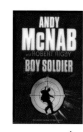

Boy Soldier
by Andy McNab and Robert Rigby Corgi €9.25

Ex-SAS man, Andy McNab, has drawn on all his experience to co-author this exciting book featuring young Danny Watts and his search for his grandfather, Fergus, a disgraced SAS officer. Together they face all kinds of very real dangers. A fast paced, action packed read which is funny and engaging, it's perfect for older Anthony Horowitz fans. There are several more titles in this series, including Payback, Avenger, and Meltdown.

If you like this author you might also like Chris Ryan or Robert Muchamore.

Goodnight Mr Tom
by Michelle Magorian
Puffin €10.75

A stirring, powerful tale about a young city boy, Willie, who is sent to stay with a gruff old man called Tom in the country during World War Two. They develop a deep friendship but their happiness is shattered when Willie has to return home to London. When Willie disappears in the city, Tom is galvanised into action. Some strong and upsetting scenes (Willie is physically abused by his mother) make this book suitable for older readers. A modern classic about the nature of friendship.

Private Peaceful
by Michael Morpurgo HarperCollins €10.75

Set during World War I, this is the shocking story of how 290 soldiers were unjustly executed for cowardice, seen through the eyes of one young soldier. Thomas Peaceful follows his older brother into the army but soon finds out that it's not all he hoped it would be. He reflects on his childhood in the English countryside from the muck and disease of the trenches. Beautifully written, this is a gripping, reflective and cleverly structured book.

If you like this book, you might also like War Boy by the same author, or Gerard Whelan's War Children.

The Cherub Series
by Robert Muchamore
Hodder €9.25

I only recently discovered these action packed books featuring teen spies and I'm now completely hooked. In the first book, The Recruit, a twelve-year-old delinquent is press ganged into a special branch of the British Secret Service and has to undergo brutal training before he is sent on his first dangerous mission. A truly exciting series, with very real characters, both male and female. There's even the odd teen romance to keep readers interested. My thirteen-year-old boy eats them up.

A must for all fans of Chris Ryan, Andy McNab or James Patterson.

Sabriel ★
by Garth Nix
HarperCollins €10.75

I'm not a huge fantasy reader but I loved this book. Sabriel is a brilliant character, a clever, brave and emotionally strong teenager. She finds out that her father, a famous magician, has disappeared and she must take over his job, banishing the undead back to the nether world and making the terrifying journey into the land of the undead to save his life. A dramatic, gripping and involving book. The kind of book that you'll always remember, whatever age you are.

Also by this author: *Lirael; Abhorsen*

Daisy Chain War
by Joan O'Neill   Hodder €9.25

Reviewed by Aoife, Dubray Books, Dun Laoghaire

Lizzie Doyle is the heroine of the first in a trilogy set in Dublin during the 1940s and the 1950s. World War Two is raging throughout Europe and, although Ireland remains neutral, there are still many hardships to be faced by the Doyle family. Ten-year-old Lizzie is trying to adjust to the 'Emergency' and then her wild cousin, Vicky, arrives from England. She's a flirt, devious and bossy. Can she and good natured Vicky ever be friends? A charming book.

Also by this author: *Daisy Chain Wedding; Daisy Chain Dream*

Hatchet
by Gary Paulsen   Macmillan €7.70

Set in the Canadian wilderness, this is the story of fourteen-year-old Brian, the sole survivor of a plane crash and how he manages to stay alive. At first he makes a lot of mistakes as he tries to find food, build a shelter and protect himself from wild animals. But in time his body and mind start to adapt to his surroundings. Not as fast paced as a Horowitz or a McNab, this book would suit a thoughtful reader who is interested in nature and survival.

If you like this book, you might also like *Kensuke's Kingdom* by Michael Morpurgo.

Eragon
by Christopher Paolini   Corgi €10.75

Eragon discovers a dragon's egg near his home. When strange figures come to look for the newly hatched dragon and destroy his home, Eragon goes on a quest to seek revenge. Along the way he meets new friends, Brom the storyteller, the mysterious Murtagh and lots of magical elves. An action packed book full of magic and set in a wonderfully imagined fantasy world.

Also by this author: *Eldest*

All About Siobhán Parkinson

MY 5 FAVOURITE BOOKS FOR CHILDREN AND WHY I LIKE THEM

1/ A LITTLE PRINCESS by Frances Hodgson Burnett – Well, as children say to me, 'I just LIKE it'!

2/ JENNINGS (and the sequels) by Antony Buckeridge – SO funny you can get a pain from laughing.

3/ THE SECRET ISLAND by Enid Blyton – Not a book to be enjoyed in adulthood, but as a child I adored this. It was the idea of the children living an independent life and the details of their food and living arrangements that enchanted me.

4/ THE TALE OF DESPEREAUX: BEING THE STORY OF A MOUSE, A PRINCESS, SOME SOUP, AND A SPOOL OF THREAD by Kate Dicamillo. If the title doesn't do it for you, don't bother to read it, but for those who get it, it is a fabulous book, in every sense.

5/ THE CATALOGUE OF THE UNIVERSE by Margaret Mahy – Just too beautiful to talk about.

5 THINGS YOU MIGHT NOT KNOW ABOUT ME

1/ My favourite food is vegetables: roasted parsnips, mashed turnip with pepper and butter, onions, grilled red peppers, stewed Jerusalem artichokes, cauliflower cheese, spinach with nutmeg … they all make me drool!

2/ I am learning Chinese. (Don't ask!)

3: My grandfather was a guard, and when I was a child I really believed him when he said he could lock me in jail in the coal cellar in his house. I have never got over it. (He was a nice man, but you wouldn't guess from this story, would you?)

4/ I HATE going to the hairdresser. I would rather visit the dentist.

5/ I once made a fried egg out of a blue plastic toy teacup by melting the cup and moulding the plastic into a flat shape and then painting it white and yellow. I have no idea why. Don't try this at home. Your skin comes off and the blue shows through the paint anyway so it doesn't work. That was the end of my artistic career.

Sisters … No Way!
(A Robert Dunbar Choice)
by Siobhán Parkinson
O'Brien Press €7.95
Reviewed by Robert Dunbar

Written in the form of two diaries, this highly entertaining and very clever story tells of how two teenager girls are forced into living with one another when the father of one of them decides to marry the mother of the other. There are some very amusing insights into contemporary teenage life and the curious ways in which some families insist on behaving!

Also by this author: Blue Like Friday; Something Invisible; Call of the Whales; The Moon King; The Love Bean

Freak the Mighty
by Rodman Philbrick
Usborne €9.25

A compelling and redeeming book about true friendship and being different, a must for any reader who likes their books quirky, funny and a little bit gritty. People are afraid of Maxwell Kane because he's slightly slow and huge but also because his father is in jail for killing his mother. But Kevin, who has a rare genetic disease making him tiny, sees past all this and they become close friends. I know it sounds a little odd, but trust me, it's wonderful.

Also by this author: *The Lobster Boy; The Fire Pony*

Wintersmith
by Terry Prachett
Corgi €10.75

Tiffany Aching is a thirteen-year-old apprentice witch. When the God of Winter falls in love with her, she enlists the help of the Wee Free Men – her tiny, crazy friends – to stop the world being frozen forever. An energetic mix of mad cap fantasy and comedy. Fans of Prachett will not be disappointed by this Discworld book. If you haven't discovered this new Tiffany Aching series yet, start with *The Wee Free Men* and *A Hat Full of Sky*.

Survival (Alpha Force Series)
by Chris Ryan
Red Fox €9.25

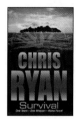

There are so many more books to keep boys reading these days, for which, as a parent and a children's bookseller I am truly grateful! Ryan, like Andy McNab, is a former member of the SAS and uses his knowledge and insight in these fast paced adventure books. The Alpha Force is a highly trained group of teen spies who can outfight with their martial arts and outwit with their code-breaking and computer hacking skills.

Pirates!
by Celia Rees   Bloomsbury € 9.25

A swashbuckling and juicy historical adventure novel set in eighteenth century Bristol, by a very talented writer. The heroine, Nancy, is shipped off to Jamaica after her father's death and is shocked when she finds out her family has made its money through slavery. She decides to join an outlawed pirate crew and discovers new friends, love and finally, democracy. Exciting, jaunty and well plotted, a dramatic pirate tale for any lovers of a good yarn.

Also by this author: *Witch Child; Sorceress*

Bec
by Darren Shan HarperCollins €9.25

I'm not a horror fan but I do admire Darren Shan's writing, most especially his vivid and rather gory (and funny at times) fight scenes, and his realistically drawn characters. His books are not for the squeamish. Bec is a trainee priestess who has to use her magical powers to save her people and battle the horrible Demonata. Full of thrilling twists, Bec is a must for any reader who likes a good scare. Horror at its best.

Also by this author: *Cirque du Freak; Lord Loss; Blood Beast*

Feather Boy
by Nicky Singer HarperCollins €9.25

Twelve-year-old Robert Noble is having a hard time in school. But his life changes when he meets an old lady, Edith Sorrel, who has a tragic past. Her son fell to his death from the window of their flat and she never got over it. On her request, Robert overcomes all his fears and breaks into the flat. A strong, compelling and powerful book about standing up for yourself and learning to fight back, with a very satisfying ending.

Switchers
by Kate Thompson Red Fox €7.70

Kate Thompson has won most of the children's book awards going, from the Bisto to the Whitbread. Switchers is her first book and it's a mystical, engaging story about teenagers who can switch, that is, change into other creatures. The 'switchers' band together to save the earth from the freezing winds of the ice-spewing krools. A highly original and dramatic novel, with strong, realistic characters. A good choice for fantasy readers.

Also by this author: *The New Policeman; The Last of the High Kings*

Girls in Love
by Jacqueline Wilson
Corgi €9.25

Nadine has a new boyfriend and her friend, Ellie, pretends she has one too but he's really only the nerdy and ugly boy who fell in love with her the previous summer. As well as the age-old boyfriend dilemmas, this entertaining novel touches on deeper themes, such as the loss of a parent and coming to terms with a new step-parent. As always, Jacqueline handles the issues with honesty and compassion and her characters are so realistic they jump off the page.

Also by this author: *Girls Under Pressure; Love Lessons; The Diamond Girls*

If you like Jacqueline Wilson, you might also like Hilary McKay or Siobhán Parkinson

MODERN CLASSIC

Northern Lights ★
by Philip Pullman Scholastic €10.75

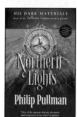

Reviewed by Anna, Dubray Books, Galway

The first part of the epic Dark Materials trilogy, *Northern Lights* has gathered rave reviews from all quarters, from avid readers of eleven to professors of philosophy, and is tipped to stand the test of generations. Twelve-year-old Lyra and her daemon, Pan, live carefree and half-wild among the scholars of Jordan College in a world much like our own – that is, until Lyra's uncle Lord Asriel, explorer and experimental theologian, visits with urgent news from the North. Soon Lyra follows, embroiled in a terrifying adventure involving stolen children, gypsies, witch-clans, armoured bears, parallel worlds and sinister scientific research. Pullman's gripping storytelling and powerful imagination also give rise to questions of a deeper nature: free will versus destiny; the nature of the soul; religion versus science; the matters of creation, evolution and death. The magnificence of the tale and its unforgettable characters will awe any reader.
Also by this author: *The Subtle Knife; The Amber Spyglass*

OTHER AUTHORS WE LOVE:

REAL LIFE/ RELATIONSHIPS:
Rachel Anderson
Terence Blacker
Rose Impey
Jaclyn Moriarty
Alex Shearer
Pete Johnson
Joan Bauer

HISTORICAL:
Kevin Crossley-Holland
Leigh Sauerwein
Marcus Sedgewick
Eleanor Updale
Karen Cushman

FANTASY/ OTHER WORLDS:
Jonathan Stroud
O.R. Melling
Robin Jarvis
Charmian Hussey
Gregory Maguire

THRILLER/ADVENTURE/ MYSTERY:
Tanith Lee
Philip Gross
Chris Wooding
Jack Higgins
Patrick Cave
Colin Bateman

WORLD ISSUES/ OTHER CULTURES:
Elizabeth Laird
Peter Dickinson
Joan Lingard
Jamila Gavin

BOOKS FOR OLDER TEENS

Older Teens

Does My Head Look Big in This?
by Randa Abdel-Fattah Marion Lloyd Books €9.25

Amal, an Australian Muslim Palestinian, struggles with her decision to wear her 'badge of faith', the hijab. Her relationship with her parents is realistically depicted, with all its teenage moments, and the joys and traumas of everyday teenage life – school, fashion, weight, phone calls and friends – are all brilliantly chronicled. A great read for teens (and adults) – funny, frank and insightful.

Go Ask Alice
by Anonymous Mandarin €10.00

Reviewed by Lynn, Dubray Books, Grafton Street, Dublin

For many teenagers, their diary is their best friend and this certainly seems true for Alice. At fifteen, she's having a rough time and the best place to put her worst fears and deepest anxieties is her diary. Alice's other escape, however, is drugs. This is a self-penned book that traces Alice's discovery of sex, drugs and dubious freedom right to the bitter end. A sad but important book for teens.

Sugar Rush
by Julie Birchill Macmillan €9.25

A sizzling, loud book about friendship, gangs and teenage love. At Revendene Comprehensive, it's survival of the fittest and Kim Lewis has to learn to cope after the safer confines of her posh private school. She finds an unlikely friend in the form of wild child, Maria, or 'Sugar', Queen of the 'Ravers'. Kim quickly falls under Maria's spell and is drawn into a world of all-night parties and heightened emotions. Has she fallen in love with her new best friend?

Forever
by Judy Blume Macmillan €9.25

This book was highly controversial when it was first published but it seems a lot less risqué today. A compelling and honest story of first love and first sex, it is written in a direct and uncompromising manner. Michael and Katherine are two teenagers who are deeply in love and have an intense relationship. Then Katherine's parents insist they put their love to the test and spend a summer apart. Written with emotional honesty, this compelling book gives real insight into teenage love, rejection, hurt and confusion. With one of the best opening lines ever.

Summers of the Sisterhood: The Sisterhood of the Travelling Pants
by Ann Brashares
Corgi €9.25

If you're feeling a little low, this is the kind of book that picks you up and gives you a great big hug. The story of four very different girls, Carmen, Lena, Bridget and Tibby, one pair of jeans ('pants' in the US) and one very special friendship. The girls must spend the summer apart but they decide to send the pants to each person in turn, by way of keeping in touch. A funny, sweet and thoughtful story of love, self-discovery and friendship.

Also by this author: *The Second Summer; Forever in Blue*

Private
by Kate Brian
Simon and Schuster €9.25

Reviewed by Helen, Dubray Books, Grafton Street, Dublin

Easton Academy is Reed Brennan's ticket away from her ordinary life and her bitter, pill-popping mother. The Billings girls are her way to the top of life at Easton Academy. But in her desperation to become one of these privileged girls, Reed realises that even having everything a girl wants doesn't mean they don't have secrets. Fans of the Gossip Girl series and TV's The OC will love this series.

Also by this author: *Invitation Only*

Junk
by Melvin Burgess
Penguin €10.75

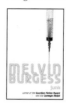

A chilling, unflinching and hard hitting tale about drug addiction. Tar and Gemma run away to the city where they get caught up in a world of drugs and crime. At first their new life together seems wild and exciting but soon Gemma's addiction takes on a life of its own. Winner of the Carnegie Medal, this thought provoking book is not for the faint hearted. But it combines strong, stark writing with a gripping plot.

Also by this author: *Sara's Face*

Road of the Dead (A Robert Dunbar Choice)
by Kevin Brooks Chicken House €10.75
Reviewed by Aoife, Dubray Books, Dun Laoghaire

This is a great novel for teenagers who aren't afraid of the dark. When their sister is found murdered, two brothers, Ruben and Cole, are determined to find out exactly what happened. Together they retrace their sister's steps to where she was found, encountering many dark and mysterious characters along the way. Ruben and Cole find themselves time and again in bad situations that just keep getting stranger. Read on…

Also by this author: *Lucas*

A Swift Pure Cry (A Robert Dunbar Choice)
by Siobhan Dowd David Fickling Books €9.25
Reviewed by Robert Dunbar

Set in Cork in 1984, this is the story of young Shell Talent, growing up in the rural Ireland of her time and learning to cope with various familial and personal difficulties, culminating in her pregnancy. The novel wonderfully evokes a time and a place and shows sympathetic understanding of the young and their problems.
Also by this author: *The London Eye Mystery (for Age 9+)*

Waves ★
by Sharon Dogar Chicken House €15.40
Reviewed by Mary, Dubray Books, Galway

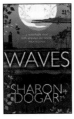

The Ditton family spend every summer basking by the sea. This year, older sister Charley is lying in a coma due to a surfing accident the previous summer. With no hope of her recovery, Charley's distraught family make the difficult decision to return to their holiday retreat. Fifteen-year-old Hal's thoughts are consumed with retracing the events that led to his sister's accident; thoughts that are not entirely his own. This is an evocative, genuine look at tragedy, relationships and life. Memorable, heart-wrenching and realistic.

If you like this, you might also like *Before I Die* by Jenny Downham

Dear Nobody
by Berlie Doherty HarperCollins €9.25

Helen is seventeen when she becomes pregnant. Her boyfriend, Chris, is about to move to college in Manchester. Helen feels completely alone and starts to write to her unborn baby, 'Dear Nobody', telling the baby her fears, hopes and confused feelings. Chris's story is told at the same time, as he reads Helen's letters, giving the reader real insight into his mixed feelings about being a father. A strong, moving and utterly compelling book which deserves to be read.

A Gathering Light ★
by Jennifer Donnelly
Bloomsbury €10.75

Winner of a Carnegie Award for children's literature, this is a wonderful book about a fifteen-year-old girl, Mattie, who longs for further education but instead must stay at home and look after her siblings. Set in a New England resort town, Big Moose Lake in 1906, Mattie's story intertwines fiction and fact, drawing on real letters written by a girl called Grace Brown, and a real life tragedy. Through Grace's letters, Mattie starts to understand her own situation. A clever, meticulously plotted book.

Forget
by Ruth Gilligan
Hodder €10.75

Ruth Gilligan was still in school when she wrote this light hearted yet thoughtful book about being a teenager in Dublin today. Eva is pretty and popular but her life changes when her Dad dies suddenly. Her one true friend, Zac, has his own problems. When Eva starts dating rugby hero, Killian, Zac isn't impressed. But will Killian eventually show his true colours and will Eva finally see sense? An engaging, topical book for all older Irish teens.
Also by this author: *Somewhere in Between*

The Year the Gypsies Came
(A Robert Dunbar choice)
by Linzi Glass   Penguin €10.75
Reviewed by Robert Dunbar

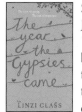

Set in the apartheid Johannesburg of the 1960s, this is the beautifully told story of the coming together of two apparently very different families, showing how their personal tragedies link them with what is going on in the countryside outside their windows. Two sets of parents, two sons and two daughters provide the material for a fascinating and deeply moving novel.

Thursday's Child
by Sonya Hartnett   Bloomsbury €10.75

Winner of the Guardian Award in 2002, this is a remarkable, powerful book about childhood. From the very first sentence – 'Now I would like to tell you about my brother, Tin' – it sucks you in. The narrator, Harper Flute, now twenty one, is looking back at her childhood in rural Australia during the Great Depression, when her brother, Tin, lived in a series of tunnels under the earth and eventually protected and saved the family. Highly original and deeply moving, a must read.
Also by this author: *The Silver Donkey*

Looking for Alaska
by John Green   HarperCollins €10.75

Robert Dunbar recommended this wonderful book to me. Set in an American college, it is a gritty, funny and engrossing read, with a truly authentic teenage voice. Miles Halter, a seventeen-year-old with no friends, dreams of starting again at his new Alabama prep school. He falls in with the Colonel and the mysterious and exotic Alaska Young and in the space of 128 days learns hard lessons in love, life, loyalty and, ultimately, death. This is an outstanding coming of age novel. I couldn't put it down.
If you like this, you might also like *Finding Violet Park* by Jenny Valentine.

Across the Nightingale Floor (Tales of the Otori, Book 1)
by Lian Hearne   Macmillan €10.75

Reviewed by Anna, Dubray Books, Galway

Set in a Japan-like land in feudal times, this is an exquisitely written, utterly gripping tale. Teenager Tomasu is one of the Hidden, a spiritual and peace-loving people. When his village is destroyed and he's rescued and adopted by Lord Otori Shigeru, he discovers that his father belonged to the Tribe, a network of assassin clans with unearthly skills – and that he shares their abilities. The land is in upheaval: war is imminent, intrigue and danger abound and love, too, beckons.

Also by this author: *Grass for His Pillow (Book 2); The Brilliance of the Moon (Book 3); and their sequel, The Harsh Cry of the Heron.*

That Girl
by Claire Hennessy   Poolbeg €9.99

'I am not normally a neurotic person.' So begins this short but compelling book about being sixteen. Dubliner Claire Hennessy started writing novels in her early teens and hasn't stopped. This book is about Kim and her anxieties about turning sixteen and having a birthday party. Her confused, conflicting feelings are examined in an honest and witty manner. Like newer author, Ruth Gilligan, Claire documents to great effect what it's like to be a teenager in Ireland today.

Mates, Dates Series
by Cathy Hopkins   Piccadilly €10.75

Nesta, TJ, Izzie and Lucy are four best friends who come from very different backgrounds. In this popular series, they help each other come to terms with boys, peer pressure, bullying and all kinds of family problems. Written in an honest, frank manner, the series is funny, moving and thought provoking. Ideal for fans of Georgia Nicholson's diaries or older Jacqueline Wilson fans.
If you like this author you might also like: Sue Limb or Rosie Rushton.

Slam
by Nick Hornby
Puffin €16.99
(€10.75 p/bk from April 08)

'One risk. One mistake and my life would never be the same…'

Have you ever wondered what it would be like to see your own future?' An entertaining and unusual story about a teenage love affair and its consequences. Told from a skateboarding-obsessed boy's point of view, it's a realistic account of the fear and downright bravery needed when facing a teenage pregnancy. There's no happy ever after ending, but Hornby uses a very novel approach to show there is always hope.

Beast
by Ally Kennen
Scholastic €10.75

A gritty story with real heart. Stephen is in foster care and he's also in trouble with the police. To make things worse, his father is a drunk, his absent mother is a 'nutter' and he's hiding a huge twelve foot primeval beast in a cage in the local reservoir. Stephen is a boy with many secrets but the Beast is certainly the biggest and the most worrying. A wry, funny and original story about an unlikely modern day hero.
Also by this author: *Berserk*

Exchange
(A Robert Dunbar Choice)
by Paul Magrs
Simon and Schuster €10.75

Reviewed by Robert Dunbar

Sixteen-year-old Simon, an orphan, shares a fanatical love of books with his grandmother. This takes them to the Great Big Book Exchange second-hand bookshop, the starting point for a very engaging story which impressively links literature and life and makes the reader think about the 'exchange' which operates between them.

Twilight ★
by Stephanie Meyer
Atom €10.75

Reviewed by Helen, Dubray Books, Grafton Street, Dublin

When Isabella Swan moves to gloomy Forks, it's just as bad as she thought it would be. Then she meets the alluring Edward Cullen, who seems to take an immediate dislike to her, and she discovers his secret. Readers of horror and romance will love this story; Meyer's lyrical writing will suck them in until they've reached the final page. And then they'll reach for her next book, New Moon.
Also by this author: *Eclipse*

Small-Minded Giants
by Oisín McGann   Corgi €9.25

It's the twenty-third century, temperatures have plummeted to sub-Arctic levels and a whole civilisation is living crammed in one city, Ash Harbour. This is the compelling story of one Ash Harbour teenager, Solomon Wheat, a sixteen-year-old with very adult problems. When his father, Gregor, disappears, accused of murder, 'Sol' tries to discover the truth about a sinister gang called the Clockworkers in the hope of finding him. Good, solid entertainment which will delight any science fiction fan.

Set in Stone
by Linda Newbery
David Fickling Books €9.25

An atmospheric page turner set in the late 1800s. Samuel Godwin, a young artist, accepts a job with the wealthy Mr Farrow to teach art to his daughters, Juliana and Marianne at their huge house, Fourwinds. All is not as it seems; lies, betrayal and murder lie at the very centre of the house. Samuel is frightened but also intrigued by the mystery. Can Charlotte, the governess help him? An unusual and compelling novel for thoughtful readers.
Also by this author: *Sisterland*

Good Omens
by Terry Pratchett and Neil Gaiman
Corgi €12.30

At the start of this book, a small boy is playing with his dog in the countryside. Then we realise the boy is the Antichrist, the dog is the hound of hell and Armageddon is fast approaching. A complex, compelling, and highly entertaining fantasy by two giants of the genre, Terry Pratchett (Discworld novels) and Neil Gaiman (Coraline and the Sandman comics). Brilliant stuff for older teens who like something with a bit of bite.

Angus, Thongs and Full-Frontal Snogging
by Louise Rennison   Scholastic €9.25

This is the diary of Georgia Nicholson, a delightfully funny and honest teenager. If your teenager likes a good belly laugh, this is the ideal book. It is about her life, her cat, Angus, and the men in her life, who drive her mad. She has a lot of problems, like how can she cope with the challenging business of snogging without any practice? Luckily there's a boy in the neighbourhood who will give private lessons. Sheer entertainment.
Also by this author: *Startled by His Furry Shorts; It's OK, I'm Wearing Really Big Knickers*

How I Live Now
(A Robert Dunbar Choice)
by Meg Rosoff   Puffin €10.75
Reviewed by Robert Dunbar

One of the most highly praised young adult novels of recent years, this is the story of an American cousin arriving into the lives of a British family and, in particular, of the development of the relationship established between the narrator, Elizabeth, and cousin Edmond. Written with complete openness and candour and against a stunning background of time and place, this stylish novel breathes new life into the well-tried themes of young love and burgeoning sexuality.
Also by this author: *Just in Case; What I Was*

Maus
by Art Spiegelman
Puffin €26.15

One of the very best books about the Holocaust. Set in Poland in the 1940s, it's moving, dark, wry and painful. It's also a graphic novel or comic book, and, in a clever metaphorical twist, the Polish Jews are mice, and the Nazis trying to chase and exterminate them are cats. Two narratives run side by side, the story of Spiegelman's parents, fighting to survive, and the story of Spiegelman and his thorny relationship with his difficult father, Vladek. Extraordinary and compelling.

If you like this, you might like *Persepolis* by Marjane Satrapi, another graphic novel.

Stargirl ★
by Jerry Spinelli
Orchard €9.25

'She was home schooling gone amuck.' 'She was an alien.' 'Her parents were circus acrobats.' Sixteen-year-old Leo Borlock is fascinated by the magical Stargirl who wears a kimono to school and plays a ukulele in the cafeteria. When the pupils start to turn against her, Leo has to choose: will he go with the herd or make a stand? A beautifully written and profound book about having the guts and the courage to be yourself, no matter what it means. Unforgettable. Another writer to seek out.

Also by this author: *Loser; Eggs*

The Secret Diary of Adrian Mole Aged 13¾
by Sue Townsend
Puffin €9.25

In this frank and funny diary, Adrian Mole talks about his life, his wayward parents, his spots, his terrible poetry, bullies, Bert Baxter, a senior citizen he minds, and the small size of his 'thing'. His distinct and horribly realistic teenage voice is a tour de force and these books have entertained teens and adults for many years now. Slightly subversive and laugh out loud funny. A modern teenage classic.

A Note of Madness
by Tabitha Suzama   Definitions €9.25

Reviewed by Helen, Dubray Books, Grafton Street, Dublin

The pressure might finally be getting to Flynn, a pianist in the Royal College of Music. When his friends finally seek outside help, Flynn realises that the way he's been feeling might not be stress after all. Teenagers will relate to Flynn's struggle with self-doubt and the pressure he puts himself under. This book is an insightful and realistic novel.

All About Kate Thompson

MY 5 FAVOURITE BOOKS FOR CHILDREN AND WHY I LIKE THEM

1. THE LITTLE HUMPBACKED HORSE. I had a beautiful Soviet edition of this Russian fairy tale when I was a child. The illustrations were some of the best I've ever seen and have stayed with me to this day.

2. THE WILD WHITE STALLION by Rene Guillot. I loved this book because of the relationship between the horse and the boy. I read and re-read it, especially the tragic ending.

3. THE OWL SERVICE by Alan Garner. One of the most mysterious books ever. I read this one several times as well. Recently I had to review it and when I re-read it, I saw things I had never seen before. Still fresh and original, thirty years on.

4. THE ECLIPSE OF THE CENTURY by Jan Mark. A breath-taking work of imaginative fiction. As I was reading it, I felt as though I had entered into a dream, and the characters and images remain with me still.

5. THE WHITE DARKNESS by Geraldine McCaughrean. Wonderful characters and a great adventure story. A modern classic. (Reviewed on page 79)

5 THINGS YOU MIGHT NOT KNOW ABOUT ME

1. I'm a tea fanatic, but I hate tea-bags. You can't beat the old-fashioned cuppa with the leaves left in the bottom.

2. I walked across Ireland with a friend, fasting. This was in the early eighties when there were plans for a nuclear power station in Carnsore Point and a uranium mine in Donegal. We walked between the two places as a protest. It took us eleven days, and we didn't eat in all that time.

3. I don't have a TV. I think that watching TV is a stupendous waste of time.

4. I'm an avid cricket fan, and listen to Test Match Special on Radio 4 whenever I get the opportunity. I prefer radio to TV because I can do other things while I'm listening, like write emails and work on my fiddle repairs.

5. I walked on fire in India. I was helping out at a place called The Atheist Centre, and the fire-walking was a demonstration to prove to people that there is nothing mystical or spiritual about the practice. It was one of the scariest things I have ever done, but my feet didn't get burned.

Annan Water

(A Robert Dunbar Choice)

by Kate Thompson

Red Fox €7.70

Reviewed by Robert Dunbar

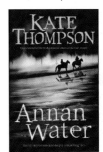

Starting off as what seems like a story mainly dealing with horses and show-jumping, this powerfully strong novel soon becomes a gripping narrative of the ecstasies and heartbreaks of adolescent love, set against the haunting refrain of a well-known traditional ballad and written in a style which memorably combines simplicity and emotion.

Elsewhere
by Gabrielle Zevin
Bloomsbury €10.75

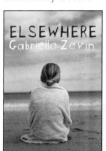

A beautifully written book about life and death and what happens next. Liz Hall, 15, is hit by a car and finds herself in a strange, dreamy world where everything seems real, yet confusingly different. It's full of warmth and character and the plot is thought-provoking and uplifting. The world Liz now lives in is so well conceived and 'real', it sends shivers up and down your spine. A wonderful book, both calm and intriguing, for thoughtful teen readers.

The Book Thief
by Markus Zusak
Doubleday €16.95

Reviewed by Vivienne, Dubray Books, Rathmines

Nine-year-old Liesel moves to a town near Munich in 1939. Her family has been unfairly taken away from her and so she feels justified in stealing the books she covets. Death, the narrator, draws us into the lives of Liesel's foster father, who teaches her to read, her best friend Rudy and the Jewish man hidden in the basement. This thought provoking story about life and love is an excellent read for teenagers and adults. A future classic.

MORE AUTHORS WE LOVE:

EDGY READS FOR THOUGHTFUL TEENS:
David Levithan
Aidan Chambers
E. R. Frank
Scott Westerfeld
Ellen Wittlinger
Laurie Helse Anderson
M T Anderson
K K Bech

WAR/WORLD ISSUES/OTHER CULTURES:
Mal Peet
Bali Rai

RELATIONSHIPS/FAMILY:
Valerie Mendes
Caroline Plaisted
Catherine McPhail
Sarra Manning
Kate Petty
Kate Cann
Anne Cassidy
Sarah Dessen
Chris Lynch

OTHER WORLDS:
David Eddings
Sarah Singleton

Something Beginning With P
by Various Authors O'Brien Press €24.95

An exceptionally well-produced poetry book featuring new poems from a host of Irish poets. Illustrated in full colour by two young Irish artists with very different styles – shifting from the painterly work of Corrina Askin to the more graphic style of Alan Clark, best known for his Ross O'Carroll Kelly illustrations. The book has deservedly won many trade and literary awards. Something a bit different. Age six plus.

Where We Were Very Young
by A A Milne; illustrated by E H Shephard
Egmont €10.75

A A Milne, author of the Winnie the Pooh stories, also wrote charming children's poetry which is gentle and nostalgic, with lots of 'nursery teas'. They are ideal for reading aloud to toddlers and young children and bridge the gap between nursery rhymes and 'proper' poetry. They are sweetly old fashioned and the illustrations by E H Shephard (who also illustrated Winnie the Pooh) suit the text perfectly. Age three plus.
Also by this author: *Now We Are Six*

There's an Awful Lot of Weirdos in Our Neighbourhood
by Colin McNaughton Walker Books €7.70

From Nosy Parker to Lemmy the Driver and Crazy Frankie, this large format book is crammed with crazy characters and guaranteed to raise a giggle or two. With bright, child friendly cartoon-style illustrations by the author, there are poems, raps and rhymes that are great for reading aloud at home or in a classroom. An ideal choice for children who like ghosts, monsters and a good laugh. Age four plus.

Please, Mrs Butler
by Allan Ahlberg
illustrated by Fritz Wegner
Puffin €10.75

This is a classic children's poetry collection. Ahlberg draws on his years as a teacher to produce charming, witty and thought-provoking poems about school and all it entails. Parents will laugh at the poems about teacher's dilemmas; children will recognise themselves in the poems about best friends, school trips and playground games. Again, great for reading aloud. Age five plus.
Also by this author: *Heard It in the Playground*

INFORMATION BOOKS FOR ALL AGES

These days, information books are packed with illustrations, photographs and graphics to hold the attention of even the most internet-savvy child. There is something for every child and every interest. Three publishers in particular merit a mention: Dorling Kindersley, Usborne and Scholastic.

Dorling Kindersley are masters of the glossy hardback, packed with colourful photographs; Usborne specialise in accessible paperbacks covering most things under the sun, from sharks to learning Irish; and Scholastic have made history fun with their hugely popular Horrible History series by Terry Deary.

REFERENCE BOOKS

Every child should have access to a good dictionary, encyclopedia and atlas and all of our shops stock a range of different books to suit your child (and your pocket). The Oxford range of dictionaries is particularly good.

DICTIONARIES

There are many different reference books in the Oxford range, from the *Oxford Very First Dictionary* (€15.40) to the *Oxford Children's Dictionary* for older children. Good, solid, reliable books. There are also a Thesaurus and a Rhyming Dictionary (€12.30 each) for any budding writers or poets in your midst.

ENCYCLOPEDIAS

One of our favourite reference books is the *DK Children's Illustrated Encyclopedia* (€45.16). It has thousands of entries and is packed with photographs and maps, making it a pleasure to browse through. With eight hundred pages of information, it's a must for any family. There are also Encyclopedias of Science, Space, and the Human Body, (€23.10 each) all excellent books.

ATLASES

DK also have some wonderful atlases, from the *Picture Atlas* (€20.00), to the wonderful *Children's World Atlas* (€23.10), and the amazing *Night Sky Atlas* (€23.10) for any budding star spotters. As children grow older, they become more and more interested in the world around them and a good Atlas is essential. And speaking of stars, for a handy little paperback guide to the night sky, you can't beat Usborne's *Spotter's Guide to the Night Sky* (€6.15). I've used it myself, lying on a rug, staring up at the stars in West Cork through binoculars with my son. If you haven't tried star gazing, do; it's great fun.

The *Usborne Children's Picture Atlas* (€7.70) is also an excellent resource and, for the very young, their *First Atlas* (€15.40), which is internet linked, is a good choice.

Other useful and fun books

for children who are interested in geography and travel are: *The Flags Sticker Book*, and the *Sticker Atlas of the World* (€7.70each), again by Usborne. Usborne also produce a *Jigsaw World Atlas* in the form of a jigsaw book (€12.30), which again makes learning fun and makes a nice present for a budding world traveller.

If your child is interested in learning another language, try the Usborne Languages for Beginners series of books and book and tape or CD packs. I've enjoyed using *Spanish for Beginners* (€15.40), and my son found *Irish for Beginners* (€16.95) very useful before going to Irish college.

HERE ARE MORE OF OUR FAVOURITE INFORMATION BOOKS:

Where's Wally?
by Martin Handford   Walker Books €9.25

Wally has been on the go for many years now and is still as popular as ever. A large format picture book cum puzzle adventure, the reader must pick out the tiny, hidden Wally on each crammed page. It's great fun and is also good for honing the powers of observation. I'm a big Wally fan myself but I'm not half as good at finding him as my four-year-old is! Age four plus.

If you like Wally, you might also like the Usborne Young Puzzle Adventure books.

Diary of a Young Girl: The Definitive Edition
by Anne Frank   Puffin €10.75

Reviewed by Nathan, Dubray Books, Grafton Street, Dublin

This is Anne Frank's famous account of a Jewish family hiding in a secret annexe in Nazi occupied Amsterdam. Charting two and a half years of living in fear, Anne writes honestly and openly about the trials of growing up under constant adult scrutiny, teenage love, the world she left behind and the future. Her insights into the mundane and the profound make this simple diary an extraordinary read. The Definitive Edition includes never before printed material which had been edited out by Anne's father. Age eleven plus.

Chinese Cinderella
by Adeline Yen Mah
Puffin €9.25

The stirring autobiography of a young Chinese girl who was both unwanted and unloved. Her mother died a few days after her birth and, as one of seven siblings, including two children from her father's second marriage, she was treated with contempt by all around her, apart from her beloved Aunt Baba and her grandfather. Despite her upbringing, Adeline went on to be a doctor and to have a happy marriage. This book, written from the heart, is sad yet ultimately triumphant tale. Age ten plus.

Mr William Shakespeare's Plays
by Marcia Williams
Walker Books €10.75

A great introduction to the bard's work. Each of the stories is written in comic book style, and in the borders of each page, extra characters comment on the action. The book includes Romeo and Juliet, Hamlet and Macbeth and is an excellent way of bringing these thrilling plays to life for younger readers. And if you haven't read or seen them performed for a while, it's a good refresher. Each story is about four pages long but manages to retain all the basic concepts of the plot. Very colourful cartoon illustrations. Age six plus.
Also by this author: *Greek Myths; King Arthur and the Knights of the Round Table*

Pirateology
by Dugald Steer
Templar Publishing €27.70

This glamorous looking book about pirates has envelopes with removable letters, pamphlets, a coded treasure map, and other lift-the-flap discoveries on every page. It also has a wealth of solid and diverse historical information, as well as a fictional pirate's journal. The illustrations are also highly detailed and fun to pore over. A must for swashbuckling children of age five plus.
Also in this series: Egyptology

The Dangerous Book for Boys ✶
by Conn and Hal Igguiden
HarperCollins €30.75

This brilliant book is packed with all kinds of useful information and things to do. From how to wrap a parcel with brown paper and string and how to make a tree house, to fourteen pirate flags and the men who sailed under them, and books every boy should read (including Roald Dahl, A A Milne, Mark Twain, E B White and Stephen King), this book is a must for any self respecting boy, young or old. Even includes tips on impressing girls. Age eight plus.

101 Things to Do Before You're Old and Boring
by Richard Horne and Helen Szirtes Bloomsbury €9.25

I hadn't paid much attention to this book until my thirteen-year-old son said I had to include it. As he has filled in the section on pretending to be ill convincingly (tummy bug – 1 day off school) and given himself a gold star, I think he may live to regret it. It's basically a book of 101 cool, interesting and slightly subversive (see above) things to do: from sending a message in a bottle, to juggling and reading. Odd, hilarious and strangely addictive. Age twelve plus.

ART AND HOBBIES

The Art Book for Children
Phaidon €19.90

A large, glossy book containing information about thirty different artists, from Gilbert and George to Botticelli, Van Gogh to Andy Warhol, along with excellent reproductions of their most famous works of art. The gentle, insightful questioning in the text encourages children to really look at and think about art for themselves. There are also activities to try out, like Miro's idea of trying to draw simple shapes like a star, blindfolded. A good book to share with children of an arty disposition.

The Doodle Book: Draw! Colour! Create!
by Taro Gomi Thames and Hudson €15.40

I would have loved this book as a child. It's packed with dozens of different activities, from colouring and cutting and pasting to drawing a fish in a fish tank and creating zany masks. Hours of fun for children who like to doodle, and especially good for children who need a bit of an art confidence boost. The drawings and instructions start off easy (eg drawing leaves on a tree) but get progressively harder. Also very therapeutic for stressed parents.

If you like this book, you might also like *Drawing for the Artistically Undiscovered*, Klutz Books (by Quentin Blake); and *Usborne Complete Book of Drawing*.

Big Book of Things to Do
Usborne €15.40

Cooking, glueing and making presents, there's plenty of great ideas in this useful book. Age 4+

50 Rainy Day Activities
Usborne €9.25

A clever set of activity cards with lots of wet weather day ideas. Ideal for Irish holidays.
Also in this series: *50 Things to Do on a Journey*

COOKERY BOOKS

I am a huge fan of cooking with children; it is a great way to keep them occupied and it teaches them useful life skills too. It is also a fantastic way to spend some time together. Luckily there are some great children's cookery books on the market. Here are some of my favourites:

The Cooking Book
by Jane Bull
Dorling Kindersley €10.75

Jane Bull's books are always beautifully designed and packed with great things to do and her cookery book is no exception. Lots of photographs illustrate over fifty recipes for older chefs of 8+.
Also by this author: *The Crafty Art Book; The Gardening Book; The Hallowe'en Book*

Children's Step by Step Cook Book
by Angela Wilkes

Dorling Kindersley €16.95

Another great cookery book for slightly older chefs of eight plus. This is really easy to use and, again, has some great photographs to illustrate all the delicious recipes.

The Usborne First Cookbook
Usborne €20.00

A great book for the youngest chefs. Lots of bright, child friendly illustrations make this book fun to look at and to use. Age six plus.

Kid's Can Cook
by Sarah Webb

Children's Press €5.99

Yes, I'm recommending my own book but it is one of the few children's cookery books that contain Irish recipes. Plus my easy peasy recipe for banoffee (which I use all the time for dinner parties), buns, lemon cake, and lots of other delicious things. With lots of handy safety tips to keep the little ones safe in the kitchen, plus fun black and white illustrations by Terry Myler. Age six plus.

SPORTS AND HOBBIES

If your child is interested in a particular sport or hobby, there are lots of books to choose from. The Usborne Starting series is great for younger readers. The range includes Starting Riding, Starting Ballet and Starting Chess and the information is presented in a fun, interesting way, with lots of illustrations and photographs. Dorling Kindersley also have some excellent sport and hobby books including:

The Ballet Book
by Darcey Bussell

Dorling Kindersley €9.25

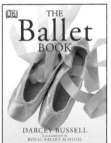

I'm a huge ballet fan and I would have loved this book as a child. Produced in association with the Royal Ballet School and written by one of the most famous English prima ballerinas (who recently retired from dancing), it is full of fascinating information on ballet, from basic positions to expert step by step advice for older dancers. Age six plus.

Also from Dorling Kindersley: *Football; Riding School; Chess*

SCIENCE AND NATURE

The Way Things Work
by Neil Ardley   Dorling Kindersley €23.10

This has long been a favourite in my house. If you live with a child who is always asking why, this is the book for you. Find out what gadgets such as the toilet, the carburettor and the fire extinguisher have in common in this heavily visual, witty guide to just about everything. If (like me) you have no idea how your telephone works, read this book. Age eight plus.

Animal ★
Edited by David Burnie
Dorling Kindersley €30.75

An amazing book. I gave this to my son for Christmas but I spent most of Christmas Day reading it myself. And I've gone back to it time and time again for information and so has my son. My four-year-old daughter is now showing interest and it is starting to look a little battle worn. But that's how a much-loved book should look.
Also in this series: *Earth; Ocean*

Watch Me Grow Series: Elephant
Dorling Kindersley €7.70

If there was a prize for the nature book with the biggest 'ah' factor, this book would win hands down. It introduces a baby elephant's eye view of the world using first person narrative and the most amazing photography. If you're looking for a book to share with a younger child who loves animals, look no further.
Also in this series: Frog; Ape; Puppy; Kitten

Eyewitness Series
Dorling Kindersley €12.30 each

This excellent series has been going strong for many years now. If you are looking for a book on a particular subject for an older child of eight plus, try this series. As there are over fifty books in the range, do ask if we don't have a title on the shelves and we will happily order it in for you. Books in the series include: *Pirate; Human Body; Knight; Viking; Dinosaur.*

DINOSAURS

Dinosaurs are always popular with children of a certain age, often boys, and there's a feast of delicious dinosaur books out there. Some of our favourites include:

Encyclopedia Prehistorica Dinosaurs: The Definitive Pop-Up
by Robert Sabuda and Matthew Reinhart
Walker Books €30.75

An amazing pop up book which brings dinosaurs to life. Age six plus.
Also by these authors:
Encyclopedia Prehistorica: Sharks and Other Sea Monsters

Visual Encyclopedia of Dinosaurs
DK €15.40

For the real dino fans! Crammed with illustrations and 'photographs'. Age eight plus.

Encyclopedia of Dinosaurs and Prehistoric Life
DK €23.10

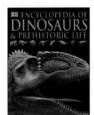

Another for real dino fans – very detailed. Over 300 pages and 700 illustrations. Age eight plus.

The Great Dinosaur Search
Usborne €7.70

A puzzle book and an information book. Spot the different dinosaurs on these packed pages. Good fun for eagle-eyed dino fans. Age four plus.

HISTORY

THE HORRIBLE HISTORY SERIES
by Terry Deary
Scholastic various prices

The Horrible History series has been going strong for many years now and is hugely popular with young history fans of seven plus. They are designed to make history fun for children, with lots of quirky cartoon drawings and fascinating facts. From The Cut Throat Celts to The Rotten Romans and The Vicious Vikings, these are great books to keep children reading. There is a Horrible History of Dublin and Ireland in the range, a must for any child who wants to find out about naked Irish warriors or old Irish curses.

Also in the Horrible series:
Horrible Science; Horrible Geography

BOOKS ON BABIES, ADOPTION, BULLYING AND OTHER SUBJECTS

Books can help children and teenagers (and their parents) explore and deal with particular occasions and emotions, like the death of a much loved grandparent or a new baby in the family. Often teenagers are curious about a particular issue even if they are not experiencing it themselves. I know as a teenager I was fascinated by GO ASK ALICE, a pretty harrowing account of drug addiction. It certainly made me more aware of the emotional issues behind addiction.

If there are subjects or issues that we haven't covered here, please do ask one of our booksellers for help. They will happily search for suitable books and order in titles that are not on the shelves.

As 'issues' go, Jacqueline Wilson has pretty much covered most of them and her books on modern families and modern friendships are thoughtful, responsible and well written. Judy Blume is another author who has covered a lot of different issues, from teenage sex (in FOREVER) to divorce.

There are lots of teenage novels which deal with emotions and contemporary themes; many are reviewed in the Age 11+ and Older Teenagers sections of this book. I have added some more suggestions on the following pages.

THE FIRST EXPERIENCES SERIES BY USBORNE

Written in simple language for young children to understand, this paperback series covers lots of different topics from The New Baby and Going to the Hospital, to Going to the Doctor (€6.15 each). The illustrations are bright and child friendly. Recommended for toddlers and younger children.

THE TOPSY AND TIM RANGE BY LADYBIRD

These small hardback books cover a whole range of topics, from The New Baby to Going to a Birthday Party. My favourite is *Topsy and Tim Have Itchy Heads*, when the twins have a nit attack (€3.85). They are ideal for toddlers and younger children of two plus.

DEATH AND BEREAVEMENT:

Michael Rosen's Sad Book ★
by Michael Rosen
illustrated by Quentin Blake
Walker Books €16.95

I can't praise this book highly enough. Searingly honest, painfully sad, but ultimately hopeful and positive, Rosen explains how he felt after his son, Eddie, died and how he dealt with and continues to deal with his deep sadness. An important book for all ages as we all get sad sometimes. It tells children that it is all right to feel this way and, importantly, that they won't always feel this way. Exceptional illustrations by Blake, best known for his Roald Dahl illustrations. Age five plus.

Bridge to Terabithia
by Katherine Paterson
Puffin €10.75

See the review on page 65.

Badger's Parting Gifts
by Susan Varley
HarperCollins €9.25

Poignant picture book about the death of an old friend. Age three plus.

All Shining in the Spring
by Siobhán Parkinson
O'Brien Press €6.34

A short book with lots of wonderful black and white illustrations. It deals with the death of a baby and is beautifully written and heart-stoppingly honest. Age four plus.

The Velveteen Rabbit
by Margery Williams
Egmont €15.40

Sweet, nostalgic story about love, loss and letting go. Age five plus.

The Cat Mummy
by Jacqueline Wilson
Corgi €7.70

See the review on page 47.

Tiger Eyes
by Judy Blume
Macmillan €9.25

About a family who are trying to rebuild their lives after the father is murdered in a robbery. Strong and thought provoking. Age eleven plus.

STARTING SCHOOL:

Starting School
by Janet and Allan Ahlberg
Puffin €7.70

A charming picture book for age two plus.

BABIES AND THE FACTS OF LIFE

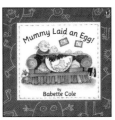  

Mummy Laid an Egg
by Babette Cole   HarperCollins €9.25

Rude, honest and very, very funny. See the review on page 32.

Facts of Life ★   Usborne €13.85

Practical, with an attractive lay out and no nonsense information. Age nine, ten or eleven, depending on the child and on how much you want them to know.

Flour Babies
by Anne Fine   Puffin €9.25

A class of boys have to look after pretend 'babies'. See the review on page 58.

What's Inside Your Tummy, Mummy?
by Abby Cocovini   Red Fox €10.75

Bright, fun look at pregnancy with lots of 'life-size' illustrations. Age three plus.

A NEW BABY IN THE FAMILY

The New Baby
by Anne Civardi
Usborne €6.15

Great little picture book for the two to five age group in the First Experiences range.

Superfudge
by Judy Blume
Macmillan €7.70

When Fudge, nearly five, discovers his new baby sister can't play with him he tries to sell her. Then he kicks his teacher and calls her 'Ratface'. But his big brother has an idea. A funny look at sibling rivalry. Warning: it has a Santa spoiler in it. Age eight plus.

POTTY TRAINING

I Want My Potty
by Tony Ross
HarperCollins €9.25

The Little Princess is potty training with hilarious consequences. The text is nice and simple for young children and the illustrations are lively and witty.

On Your Potty
by Virginia Miller
Walker Books €7.70

A picture book about a little bear who doesn't quite understand his potty.

BULLYING

The Eighteenth Emergency
by Betsy Byars Puffin €6.15

An American story about Benkie who is bullied by 'Neanderthal Man', Ezzie. A useful book for anyone who has been picked on or bullied. Age nine plus.

The Diddakoi
by Rumer Godden Macmillan €7.70

Kizzy is different, she's half gypsy and lives in a caravan. This powerful, well written book explores issues of racism and bullying. Age ten plus.

Stargirl (Also on peer pressure)
by Jerry Spinelli Orchard Books €9.25

See review on page 93.

Feather Boy
by Nicky Singer HarperCollins €9.25

See review on page 84.

Adam's Starling
by Gillian Perdue O'Brien Press €6.95

See review on page 45.

Bad Girls and The Dare Game
by Jacqueline Wilson
Corgi (€9.25 each)

Two excellent novels from Wilson with a bullying theme.

Also: *Matilda* by Roald Dahl; *Willy and Hugh* (picture book) by Anthony Browne

BODY IMAGE/ WEIGHT PROBLEMS

Fat Boy Swim
by Catherine Forde
Egmont €9.25

A brilliant book for anyone who cringes at the thought of PE or swimming. The first chapter captures the horror of school football to perfection. Age ten plus.

Fat Kid Rules the World
by K L Going
Corgi €7.70

 Troy is morbidly obese and knows he can never fit in. When a homeless teenager saves his life, they begin an uneasy, unusual friendship. Then they start a band together. Heart warming, funny and edgy. Age eleven plus.

Also: *Blubber* by Judy Blume

SELF HARM

Cut
by Patricia McCormick
HarperCollins €7.70

 A strong, well written account of one girl's self harm (cutting) and how she tries to heal her addiction. Age eleven plus.

EATING DISORDERS

Second Star to the Right
by Deborah Hautzig
Walker Books €9.25

A strong, well written book for teens about anorexia nervosa. On the face of it. Leslie seems a normal fourteen-year-old. She should be happy but she's not. Maybe if she was thinner… (Currently reprinting – ask your bookseller for details)

Girls Under Pressure
by Jacqueline Wilson   Corgi €9.25

Ellie feels fat compared to her friends and goes on a diet. But soon she can't stop. Another excellent novel from Wilson, dealing with a serious issue. Age eleven plus.

Also on this topic: *Massive* by Julia Bell

GENDER ISSUES

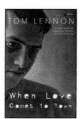

And Tango Makes Three
by Justin Richardson and Peter Parnell
Simon and Schuster €10.75

Based on a true story, this is a picture book about two male penguins who are a bit different. They are given an egg to look after and do a great job of hatching and rearing it together. Age four plus.

Allison
by Tatiana Strelkoff
O'Brien Press €7.61

When Karen meets Allison her world is turned upside down. They fall in love but what will their friends and family think? Older teens.

When Love Comes to Town
by Tom Lennon
O'Brien Press €9.95

Set in Dublin, this book is about the emotional crises faced by one gay teenager, seventeen-year-old Neil. Older teens.

Also on this topic: *Sugar Rush* by Julie Birchill – See the review on page 86.

TEENAGE PREGNANCY
(All these titles are novels for teens)

Dear Nobody
by Berlie Doherty   HarperCollins €9.25
See review on page 88.

Blue Moon and Baby Blue
by Julia Green   Puffin €9.25

Blue Moon is the first of these excellent titles about a teen pregnancy and the realities of bringing up a baby as a young mother.

Reckless
by Sue Mayfield   Hodder €7.70
Especially good on the boy's point of view.

Slam
by Nick Hornby   Puffin €16.99
See review on page 90.

DEPRESSION AND MENTAL HEALTH

A Note of Madness
by Tabitha Suzuma
Definitions €9.25

See review on page 93.

The Illustrated Mum
by Jacqueline Wilson
Corgi €9.25

A very strong, powerful book about a mum who suffers from depression and how her daughters deal with this. Age ten plus.

DRUG PROBLEMS

Junk
by Melvin Burgess
Penguin €9.25

See review on page 87.

Go Ask Alice
by Anonymous
Arrow €10.00

See review on page 86.

BED WETTING

Ed's Bed
by Eoin Colfer
O'Brien Press €5.95

See review on page 37.

FOSTERING AND ADOPTION

The Story of Tracy Beaker
by Jacqueline Wilson
Corgi €9.25

Tracy lives in a children's home and dreams that one day her mother will come back for her. But this causes problems when potential foster parents come to see her. Age 9+

Driftwood
by Cathy Cassidy
Puffin €9.25

On fostering (a teenage boy). See review on page 53.

My New Family: A First Look at Adoption
by Pat Thomas
Barrons ($5.95) can be ordered

A useful book for younger children of five plus.

SEPARATION AND DIVORCE

The Suitcase Kid
Jacqueline Wilson
Corgi €9.25

A strong, well written book about a young girl called Andrea and how she learns to cope with her parents' divorce. Age nine plus.

Hatchet
by Gary Paulsen
Macmillan €7.70

See review on page 81.

Madam Doubtfire
by Anne Fine
Puffin €9.25

Hilarious yet tender look at divorce and one very determined dad who dresses up as a woman to get the job as his own children's nanny, filmed as *Mrs Doubtfire*. Age ten plus.

BOOKS FOR PARENTS
BOOKS ABOUT CHILDREN'S BOOKS

If you'd like to find out more about particular aspects of children's books and children's reading here are some recommended titles:

The Reading Bug
by Paul Jennings
Penguin €15.40

A well respected children's author and ex-teacher explains how to keep children reading. Especially good on reluctant readers.

The Ultimate Book Guide 8–12s
The Ultimate Teen Book Guide
Both by Daniel Hahn and Leonie Flynn
A & C Black €20.00 each

Two of the best guides to older children's fiction I have ever come across. These packed books should be in every home, library and school. Literary treasure troves for parents and children can flick through the reviews and find new books they'd like to try.

Illustration reproduced by permission of Walker Books
© Niamh Sharkey from *I'm a Happy Hugglewug*

**Happy reading
from all at Dubray Books!**